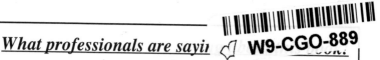

_"A superb book...It is an excellent
resource for school personnel, psychologists,
and the significant others of ADD individuals."_
—Arthur Freeman, Ed.D., ABPP, author of numerous
books on cognitive-behavior therapy,
and Chairman, Department of Psychology
at Philadelphia College of Osteopathic Medicine

_"Michele Novotni's new book offers practical and sensible
help in an area where such help is badly needed: social skills.
She writes clearly and gracefully, observes faithfully and
honestly, and suggests deftly and wisely."_
—Edward Hallowell, M.D., co-author of
"Driven to Distraction"

_"Strongly recommended for adults whose attentional problems
have impacted upon their abilty to understand and respond to
everyday social signals. Immensely valuable to parents,
friends, professionals and spouses of AD/HD adults."_
—Richard Lavoie, M.Ed., Host, "F.A.T. City" and "Last One
Picked...First One Picked On"

_"A much needed practical tool that can
benefit many different kinds of learners. All
people have strengths and weaknesses and
this attends to those often shared by children as well
as adults who have many ADD characteristics."_
—Lynn Weiss, Ph.D., author of "ADD in Adults"

Social Skills Help for Adults with
Attention Deficit/Hyperactivity Disorder
(AD/HD)
A Reader-Friendly Guide

What Does Everybody Else Know That I Don't?

Michele Novotni, Ph.D.
with Randy Petersen

Specialty Press, Inc.
300 N.W. 70th Ave.
Plantation, Florida 33317

Library of Congress Cataloging-in-Publication Data

Novotni, Michele.
    What does everybody know that I don't?: social skills for adults with attention deficit-hyperactivity disorder (AD/HD): a reader-friendly guide / Michele Novotni with Randy Petersen.
        p. cm.
    Includes bibliographical references and index
    ISBN 1-886941-34-3
    1. Atteniton-deficit disorder in adults. 2. Attention-deficit-disordered adults. I. Petersen, Randy. II. Title.

RC394.A85 N68 1999
616.85'8903--dc21
                                                                99-045492

Illustrations by Richard Dimatteo
Cover Design by David Carlson
Copyedited by Dara Kates

10 9 8 7 6 5 4 3 2 1

Printed in the United States of America
Specialty Press, Inc.
300 Northwest 70th Avenue, Suite 102
Plantation, Florida 33317
(954) 792-8100 • (800) 233-9273
www.addwarehouse.com

Contents

Acknowledgments

I am thankful for the many people who have helped to influence, support, and encourage me. I would like to especially recognize and thank the following for their contributions to *What Does Everybody Else Know that I Don't?*

Randy Petersen for using your writing talents to help make this book "reader-friendly."

My publisher, Harvey Parker, who remained amazingly calm and supportive throughout the entire publication process. It's been a pleasure working with you!

I am very grateful to Susan Sussman, Peggy Ramundo, Kate Kelly, Linda and Ed Barniskis, Kathleen Kelly, and Sheldon Nix for your thoughtful and often thought provoking review of the manuscript. Your insights and ideas were most welcome and greatly enhanced the book.

Eastern College for providing institutional support, Hilary Archer, Lynn Watts, and Trisha Reilly my graduate assistants, who collected and reviewed the research for this project, and Vangie Jackson, for providing office support.

Susan Sussman for sharing your expertise and contributing the chapter on coaching.

Harry and Wilma Thompson for use of your computer while I spent the summer in North Carolina.

Jerry Mills for permission to include your song, *Impulse*.

My parents, Bill and Alice Young, who never put limits on my dreams or ideas.

My husband, Bob, for your unending support and encouragement, and my sons, Duane and Jarryd, for their support and enthusiasm.

Many, many thanks!!!

Michele Novotni
August 1999

Dedication

*This book is
dedicated to my son Jarryd.
Through your eyes, I have come to
understand the struggles and triumphs of AD/HD.*

vi

Introduction

JARRYD SAT BY the phone waiting for it to ring. It was Saturday, and he had hoped to play with someone. Though he had called several children he knew, everyone gave some reason not to play with him. Yet one boy, John, had said that maybe he would play with Jarryd later and that he would call if he could.

Excitedly and expectantly, Jarryd waited by the phone for the call. He waited and waited, but the phone never rang. After 30 minutes I suggested that perhaps John did not really want to play but that maybe he was just trying to be nice. Jarryd rejected that possibility and continued to wait by the phone. After an hour, I suggested that it might be best to make other plans. Jarryd insisted that John was going to call back to play.

He waited and waited, staring at the phone. Another hour passed and I needed to console a very upset 10-year-old who didn't understand why people said things they didn't mean. I was overwhelmed by my son's dejection as he tried to interact socially with others.

Jarryd, my son, has been one of my best teachers. His struggle with Attention Deficit/Hyperactivity Disorder (AD/HD) awakened me to the needs of many adults with the same struggle. This sparked my first book, *Adult ADD: A Reader-Friendly Guide to Identifying, Understanding, and Treating Adult Attention Deficit Disorder.* As I journeyed through the maze of AD/HD information not only as a clinician, but also as a concerned parent, I realized a simple fact. People with AD/HD, especially adults, needed more information—they needed practical information in a format they could easily read.

My young son knew he had a problem. What he and many others like him needed to know was what to do. That's what Jarryd and the many adults with AD/HD in my life have taught me: the need for practical help.

Now Jarryd has taught me another important aspect of AD/HD, one that's often overlooked by the experts. Although Jarryd was doing well in school, I began to notice that something was missing. There was an absence of phone calls for Jarryd, an absence of children coming over to play, and an absence of invitations to sleep-overs or birthday parties. Jarryd lacked social relationships outside our family.

The teachers in Jarryd's school did not notice him committing any obvious violations of social protocol, but there clearly was something that kept other children away from him outside the classroom. Although the teacher tried to reassure me that there was no problem, she agreed to conduct an experiment with her class. The students were asked to write down the two people that they would most like to work with on a project. This information was the foundation of a sociogram, a drawing that illustrates a group's social connections. The results confirmed my suspicion. No one had chosen Jarryd! Not one child in his class of 26 had chosen to be with Jarryd! Something was wrong. Something was very wrong.

I began to notice a common thread among those I knew with AD/HD. My father, who has AD/HD, has always had very few friends. And many of my clients with AD/HD shared similar stories: difficulties with relationships at home, at work, and at play, causing a great deal of emotional pain. Many of the adults I worked with had been divorced, sometimes more than once. Many were self-employed because they found it difficult to work with others. Basically, social difficulties seemed to be everywhere in the world of AD/HD.

I decided to review the literature and determine the best treatment strategies for improving social skills for those with AD/HD. It surprised me how little information existed on this topic. And the few studies that were available showed a general lack of success in treatment. This launched my journey to explore methods of improving social skills for those who have AD/HD. My many years as a behavior management specialist paid off as I experimented with various strategies. You are reading the results of that journey. The ideas and strategies I have pulled together have helped many of my adult clients with AD/HD, and you'll read some of their stories. All the stories in this book are real, based on what people have told me about their lives. But to protect their confidentiality, I have changed their names and some identifying information—except in the stories of my son and my father.

I hope the ideas presented in this book will also help encourage you on your own journey. It has been great to see these ideas working, really working, to open up the social lives of many adults with AD/HD. But most importantly for me, I've also seen them work in Jarryd's life. My son is now getting invited to birthday parties and the phone is ringing.

How to Read this Book

Do you get frustrated by books that try to give you helpful information but are impossible to read? Maybe the language is too scientific or the explanations too theoretical. If you have AD/HD, you know how hard it is to focus on page after page of unbroken text.

This book is different. For one thing, it's chock-full of stories showing the theories *at work* in the lives of real people. And all of the stories and illustrations are italicized. If you find such stories to be unapplicable, you can simply skip those sections moving directly to the next section of text. If you enjoy the stories and find them to be helpful, you can move directly to the stories, skipping text as needed.

Each chapter ends with a section called "JUST THE FACTS," which recaps the highlights in bullet form. In addition, there are practice exercises in many sections. These are set off by a box.

For those without AD/HD, I include occasional tips to help improve the social skills for those about whom you care. These are also set off in boxes throughout the book. Finally, an index is provided at the end of the book to help you locate information you may wish to find.

Let Me Introduce Myself

I am a psychologist and educator who specializes in Attention Deficit/Hyperactive Disorder (AD/HD). I have more than 20 years of professional experience in this area and I was pulled wholeheartedly into the world of AD/HD by both my son and my father.

My son Jarryd, who is now 13, has what he calls ADRRRHD—Attention Deficit *Really Really Really* Hyperactive Disorder. My father, William Young, is in his seventies and was only recently diagnosed with AD/HD. I have learned a great deal about the struggles and triumphs of AD/HD through Jarryd and my father. In addition, I have worked with hundreds of adults and children with AD/HD in my private practice, and I have lectured to thousands regarding different aspects of AD/HD.

I co-authored *Adult ADD: A Reader-Friendly Guide to Identifying, Understanding, and Treating Adult Attention Deficit Disorder* in 1995 and currently travel around the country conducting multi-media presentations on the topic of AD/HD. With a Ph.D. in counseling psychology, I am a licensed psychologist, a certified school psychologist, and a full-time professor of counseling in the graduate program at Eastern College in Saint Davids, Pennsylvania.

And who is Randy Petersen?

Randy is a professional writer who has written or helped to write over 25 books. It was Randy who helped to make *Adult ADD: A Reader-Friendly Guide to Identifying, Understanding and Treating Adult Attention Deficit Disorder* so reader-friendly.

ADD or AD/HD?

So you've been told you have Attention Deficit Disorder (ADD). Why do we keep talking about AD/HD? Well, they're the same thing. Attention Deficit Hyperactivity Disorder (AD/HD) is now the official, clinical name for the problem. (Ironically, AD/HD doesn't always include hyperactivity.) It was renamed a few years ago; that is why you still hear people using both terms.

That's a mouthful to say, of course, and many people are not yet aware of the change. Several popular books and seminars simply call it ADD. The following are the three different kinds of ADD and their proper names:

- AD/HD—predominantly hyperactive/impulsive type: The main characteristics are hyperactivity and impulsivity.

- AD/HD—predominantly inattentive type: The main characteristics are inconsistent attention without hyperactivity.

- AD/HD—combined type: The main characteristics are hyperactivity, impulsivity, and inconsistent attention.

So because they have officially changed the name from ADD to AD/HD, I'll be using it throughout this book—just without the different subtypes.

AD/HD or ADHD?

Sometimes you may see a slash between the letters and sometimes you won't. Actually AD/HD and ADHD are both the same. It's basically a matter of preference.

JUST THE FACTS

Book format guide:
- *Italics*—stories and illustrations
- Regular print—text
- Boxed text "**JUST THE FACTS**"—chapter summary in bullet form
- Unshaded boxes—practice exercises
- Shaded boxes—Tips for those without AD/HD to help
- Index—back of book, to help locate information

Part One

Social Skills

Chapter 1

The Kindergarten Connection

WHY DOES EVERYBODY else seem to know all these rules? When were these social skills taught? Where was I when this was happening?

You may feel as if you were abducted by aliens and returned to earth with false memory implants to fill in the time gap. Although most of these gaps have been filled with some degree of accuracy, something important seems to be missing. Perhaps the aliens didn't know about human social skills either.

Or maybe it's a conspiracy. Everyone in your town had a meeting and said, "We're going to agree to follow all sorts of little rules, but don't tell *this* person." That person would be you!

But it's more likely that your difficulties with social skills are a result of the natural attention gaps—the blinks and blanks—that go along with AD/HD. As hard as you try to remember, there always seem to be gaps in your memory. Some of these gaps you can fill in later. But most children get a foundation for social skills early in life, and then they keep building on it. You may have had major gaps in your learning process at that time, and it's been difficult to catch up.

I realized this more clearly when I read a popular book by Robert Fulghum, *All I Really Need To Know I Learned In Kindergarten*. The book offers advice to adults based on simple lessons from the kindergarten years. As I flipped through the chapters, I realized that many of the lessons are actually social skills! Kindergarten is where we learn to socialize. Fulghum, in his wit and wisdom, taught many of these lessons to adults who may have forgotten them. The back cover of the book provided a great summary:

Most of what I really need to know about how to live and what to do and how to be I learned in kindergarten. Wisdom was not at the top of the graduate school mountain, but there in the sand pile at Sunday School. These are the things I learned:

- Share everything.
- Play fair.
- Don't hit people.
- Put things back where you found them.
- Clean up your own mess.
- Don't take things that aren't yours.
- Say you're sorry when you hurt somebody.
- Wash your hands before you eat.
- Flush.
- Warm cookies and cold milk are good for you.
- Live a balanced life—learn some and think some and draw and paint and sing and dance and play and work every day some.
- Take a nap in the afternoon.
- When you go out into the world, watch out for traffic, hold hands, and stick together.
- Be aware of wonder.[1]

Here on the bestseller rack was a treasure trove of social skills desperately needed by those with AD/HD. Some of the observations are more about personal growth than getting along with others, but in his simple language, Fulghum identified a number of those mysterious social skills. Let's look at a few.

Share everything.

In kindergarten, sharing involved toys such as dolls and jacks. Grown-ups have different toys—cars and stereos and lawn mowers—and these too can be shared. You may not have particular trouble sharing stuff—if you can find it. But it's also important to share your time, which may be more difficult.

Taking turns can be difficult for those who are impulsive or hyperactive. It can be difficult to wait while someone else is taking a turn, whether you're playing a video game, in a bank line, or choosing a TV show to watch.

"Let's go to the movies tonight," Duane said excitedly.

"Okay," replied Shirl. "But this time I'd like to see a romantic comedy."

"No way!" Duane demanded. "Let's go see that new action film. I really want to see it!"

"But we always see action films. This time let's see what I want to see."

Duane wouldn't budge, despite Shirl's pleading tone. "But I don't want to see a romantic comedy. I want to see the action film."

"All right," Shirl sighed. "We'll see what you want to see. Again."

Although Duane won the movie selection debate, he lost points with Shirl. Relationships involve give and take. His partner was clearly becoming frustrated with this one-sided relationship. You may be unaware of the impact of your actions on relationships. Developing an awareness of others can be difficult, but it's part of the sharing process.

You also need to share speaking time. Your conversations may more closely resemble *monologues* rather than *dialogues*. Some talk on and on, without stopping for others to exchange their ideas, often having no clue you're the only one speaking. You may not be aware that you're not sharing conversation time.

Imagine a see-saw. It would not be much fun if one person was always up and the other was always down. The fun of the see-saw is in the up and down, the give and take. Half of the interesting ideas are in the other person's head, and you need to listen to hear them.

The same see-saw principle applies to any aspect of a relationship. You can't always get your way. If you don't share time, conversation, decisions, or possessions, others will generally attribute your actions to your self-centeredness and/ or indifference toward them. That may not be your intention, but that's the message they'll receive from your actions.

Play fair.

Many kindergarten teachers have intervened during recess when a distressed child sobs, "She's not playing fair!"

Playing fair requires two basic elements:
1. Awareness of the rules.
2. Following the rules.

Playing fair doesn't seem like it should be so hard, but often it is for adults with AD/HD. Sometimes you don't play fair because you are unaware of the rules. In many games, the rules are not written—they are just known. Known by most people, that is. But what if you were playing a game and didn't know the rules? You might break the rules just because you were unaware of them.

Unfortunately, social judgments are just as harsh for those who violate the rules unknowingly as they are for willful offenders. As the adage says, "Ignorance of the law is no excuse." You are expected to know the rules! After all, everyone else does!

But sometimes you know the rules and don't follow them. Due to your impulsive or hyperactive behavior, you may get tired of waiting for your turn. Or you may find it too hard to follow the rules. Sometimes you take short cuts.

Or maybe you just want to win at any cost. You may be willing to bend or break the rules to give yourself an edge. You may not have fully considered the consequences of your actions.

As in kindergarten, people who don't play fair are often excluded from future games. Social isolation is frequently the result. But it could be worse. In the Old West, those who didn't play fair at poker were killed! Social isolation is a problem—not as bad as being shot but a problem nonetheless. It's important to know the rules and follow them.

Don't hit people.

Everyone needs to learn to manage your anger. And when you're angry, you must never hit anyone. Kindergarten kids are often sent to "time out" for hitting, or perhaps to the principal's office. As an adult, it's more likely that you'll have the police at your door or a lawsuit filed against you. You might even go to jail. Hitting is that bad!

Living with AD/HD can be frustrating—there's no question about it. Just getting dressed and getting to work on time can be an exhausting feat. There is daily tension, and there may not be many friends around to help ease the burden. As a result, internal pressure can build until you feel ready to explode.

If a pot is already full of scorching water, it does not take much additional heat for the water to boil. And you may already live near the boiling point. Any additional frustration can set you off.

That's why it's crucial for you to develop coping skills. You have to find a way to ease the pressure, to calm yourself down, especially if you're prone to aggressive outbursts. AD/HD makes you susceptible to anger, but it's no excuse for hurtful behavior. Find your outlets. Punch a pillow, leave the room, go for a walk, listen to soothing music, keep a top ten list of good things about your life. Get professional help if needed. Psychologists, counselors, or psychiatrists can help you learn effective ways to improve your coping skills and better manage your anger.

Put things back where you found them.
Clean up your own mess.
Flush.

I'll lump these together because they all basically involve picking up after yourself. No one likes to clean up after someone else—especially not able-bodied adults. Even in kindergarten one of the first rules taught is to put away your toys.

Adults with AD/HD can be great mess makers. There's a thrill in beginning to work on a project. As time passes (and sometimes with AD/HD it isn't much

8

time), interest in the project fades. But with equal zeal, a new idea is on the horizon. New items are put on the table to work on once again. The old items are pushed aside, put on a pile to be worked on or put away later.

Along with the *other* old items that were put on another pile to be worked on or put away later.

*Along with the **other** even older items that were put on yet another pile to be worked on or put away later.*

You get the idea.

This issue may affect many areas of your life, including relationships. Many marriage counseling sessions have been spent on the topic of picking up after yourself. Frustration mounts as one partner feels used and taken advantage of by the other. Accusations fly in heated arguments regarding personal responsibility. Some sound like this:

"You never put your dirty socks and underwear in the hamper!"

"You never put the milk back when you're finished with it!"

"You never do the dishes!"

And the ultimate:

"You left the seat up!"

"You didn't flush!"

Take care of your personal responsibilities. Others may find it difficult to be around you, especially intimately involved with you, if you're not accepting responsibility for yourself and your belongings.

Don't take things that aren't yours.

Sometimes in kindergarten it may be difficult to resist the temptation to take something you want. The impulse needs to be squashed. Moral reason and logic need to take over.

I might want it but it's not mine.
I must not take things that do not belong to me.
If I take that, I'll get in trouble.
If I take that, the person who owns it will be upset.

Most of us learn early in life to resist the temptation to take things that don't belong to us. Some, however, do not. The punishment gets progressively worse, from trips to the principal's office, to suspension from school, to a date in juvenile court. And adults face more serious consequences.

For those of you who struggle with poor impulse control, it may be hard to squash the desire to take something that does not belong to you. It can be tough to think through the consequences of actions when faced with the desired object. If you struggle with the impulse to take things that aren't yours, please consider getting professional help.

Say you're sorry when you hurt somebody.

Adults with AD/HD may say and do impulsive things that hurt others' feelings. You may not realize at first what damage you've caused. You also might not realize at other times that you've hurt someone's feelings. But when you do, it is important to take responsibility for your words and actions and offer an earnest apology.

A sincere apology is powerful. However, repeated violations will need some action behind the words. People are usually forgiving as long as it seems likely that they won't be hurt again. But people will rarely remain in relationships if the hurtful behavior continues.

A good apology has several facets:

1. *Becoming aware of the hurt.*

   This is often the hardest part for those with AD/HD. Try to be more sensitive to the reactions of those around you. Watch for clues in the body language and faces of others to help you notice if you have hurt someone.

2. *Taking responsibility for the hurt.*

   An apology only works if you're willing to admit you caused the pain. Own up to what you've done. "I'm sorry that I hurt you," is a big step in the right direction.

3. *Sharing the hurt.*

   I can't overstate the value of the words "I'm sorry." That phrase simply means that you feel bad along with the wounded person. People need to know that you're concerned that you've hurt them.

4. *Explaining any circumstances.*

   Sometimes there are reasons for your actions, and these may cast a different light on the situation. But an explanation can't replace an apology; you still need to apologize.. "My AD/HD makes it hard for me sometimes, but I shouldn't have done this, and I'm sorry."

5. *Promising improvement.*

   People need reassurance that they won't be hurt again. With AD/HD, improvement can be a slow process. Although you may make the same mistake more than once, a sincere apology, along with efforts to improve, will help strengthen many relationships.

Wash your hands before you eat.

Personal hygiene was important in kindergarten and it still is. Poor health habits can cause physical illness and social rejection.

Often in the rush of getting ready for work, you may not leave enough time for personal hygiene matters such as brushing teeth or showering. "No one will know. I'll just use extra deodorant or perfume." But usually people do know, and they'll stay far away from you.

In kindergarten, kids will blurt out, "You smell! Get away from us." In adulthood, the message is subtler: "I'm sorry, I already have plans. Maybe some other time." Either way, it's a rejection.

Rumpled clothing can also be a problem for many with AD/HD. There's barely enough time to dress, let alone use an iron (or find it!). Unfortunately, we are often judged by appearance. If you look unkempt, people will make all sorts of assumptions about you. People say, "Don't judge a book by it's cover," but unfortunately many do. In business, hiring decisions are often made within the first few minutes of the interview, based largely on the image you present. Personal appearance is also very important in starting new relationships, whether romantic or friendly, and maintaining those relationships. Very few people want to be associated with a disheveled person.

So make time to press your clothes (or buy clothes that don't need ironing!), comb your hair, wash your hands, trim your nails, take a shower, use deodorant, and brush your teeth. Pay attention to the image you present, because you can bet that others are.

Warm cookies and cold milk are good for you. Live a balanced life—learn some and think some and draw and paint and sing and dance and play and work every day some.

Learn to nurture yourself. Purposefully add beauty, peace, and contentment to your life. Rekindle your spirit. Take time out to play. In kindergarten, children would be very upset if they had no recess. They know the value of play. But adults need to have fun, too—especially adults with AD/HD. Since so much of life is already a struggle, some of life should be fun.

Identify the activities you enjoy. Find the activities that refill your spirit. Make sure that you make time to engage in those activities daily. You'll be more productive if you take time to refuel. Nurturing yourself is good for you. Also, if you refuel, you'll be less likely to break down. Your ability to cope with life's frustrations should increase.

Take a nap in the afternoon.

Slow down.

Take time to rest.

Take time to meditate.

In kindergarten the teachers make everyone take a nap— whether you want to or not. It's a time to slow down. A time to settle. A time to rest. Often you can be tired and not even realize it. Many children fight taking a nap, then quickly fall into a restful sleep.

For those of you with AD/HD without hyperactivity, slowing down can help to give your mind a rest. It can give you a chance to not have to work so hard to follow conversations. It can be a welcome pause in a tiring day. A time to refuel.

In the whirlwind of activity that generally surrounds the person with hyperactivity, it's important to learn to settle down. Allow time for all the racing thoughts to slow down and come into focus. Quiet time restores and refreshes, giving you more energy and creativity to conquer the challenges ahead. Quiet time allows you to reflect on the importance of relationships in your life and on ways to improve them.

Although a fast train gets you to your destination quickly, the view is not great. Blurred scenery is rarely engaging. But if you slow down, often the countryside becomes very interesting. Beautiful flowers, trees, interesting houses, and people can all be seen at a leisurely pace. In the same way, resting is good for you. Your life can be more interesting when you learn to slow down.

When you go out into the world, watch out for traffic, hold hands, and stick together.

You can get hurt if you're not careful. The world presents all sorts of dangers. In kindergarten traffic was a big fear. Cars could hurt us while we were riding our bikes or crossing the street, so we had to be careful.

It was always better if we had a friend with us when we went outside to play. There was comfort in the support of others. The other set of eyes helped keep us out of trouble. The extra set of ears helped us hear warnings. Our parents usually felt better if they knew that we were not facing the world alone. We felt better, too.

For adults, traffic is just one of many fears. Adult life brings many opportunities for us to get hurt, physically or emotionally. With AD/HD, it's even a bigger minefield. The added struggles of AD/HD seem to place people in a vulnerable position. All the more reason to "hold hands" and "stick together."

14

It may be difficult for you to reach out to others. You may have been socially rejected for such a long time that you have stopped trying to relate to others. At one AD/HD workshop, I asked how people were coping socially. One man said he had found the answer: "I just avoid people! No more social skills difficulties. That works for me." But I could tell from the pain in his eyes that it was not working as well as he said. I'm guessing that he had been hurt so many times before that he was afraid to become vulnerable again.

With AD/HD it's especially important to find support. In a couples workshop, I ask participants to break into small groups and tell one another the stories of their struggles with AD/HD. Participants tell me it's one of the most valuable exercises of the whole day. They discovered they weren't alone, that others shared their feelings. Even though each story had different details, they saw a common thread that connected them. There is much healing power in feeling connected to others.

Surround yourself with people who like you. One adult with AD/HD shared his coping skill secret: "I only stay around people who like me. If someone likes me, they'll generally tolerate my social blunders. If someone doesn't like me, it seems like there is nothing I can do to change that."

There are a few organizations that provide support to adults with AD/HD.

CHADD
Children and Adults with Attention
Deficit/Hyperactivity Disorder
8181 Professional Place, Suite 201
Landover, Maryland 20785
(800) 233-4050
www.chadd.org

ADDIEN ADDULT
Information Exchange Network
P.O. Box 1701
Ann Arbor, MI 48106
(734) 426-1659
www.addien.org

ADDA
Attention Deficit Disorder Association
1500 Commerce Parkway, Suite C
Mount Laurel, NJ 08054
(856) 439-0525
www.add.org

There are also a number of psychologists, psychiatrists, and professional coaches who can provide support and encouragement.

On an informal basis, just look around you and see who you might want to hold your hand and help you.

Be aware of wonder.

One of the most enchanting things about childhood is the excitement and wonder with which a child sees life. Children often see the good, the positives in situations. Children seem to have an amazing capacity for hope.

Many adults with AD/HD have been worn down by the struggle of life. Many seem sad, depressed, or overwhelmed, and are afraid to try to reach out for enjoyment, because they've been hurt too many times.

Instilling hope can be life-saving for those with AD/HD. It can certainly improve the quality of your life. So open your eyes and appreciate the wonders all around you. Marvel at a sunset. Join that hiking club, bird watching group, a parenting class. Take up ballroom dancing, go to concerts, etc. Observe the colors in flowers, cars, and clothing. Don't let your struggles blind you to the wonder and joy of your existence. Learning to see things in a new way can give you the courage to risk trying again. Connecting with others can help restore the sense of hope in your life.

JUST THE FACTS

- According to *All I Really Need To Know I Learned In Kindergarten,* kindergarten is where we were supposed to learn many social skills. Such as:
  - Take turns/share
  - Play fair and be aware of the rules and follow the rules.
  - Don't hit others or take things that don't belong to you.
  - Clean up after yourself.
  - Apologize when you hurt someone.
- Personal hygiene is important.
- Learn to nurture yourself. Learn to slow down and relax.
- Connect with others with AD/HD through support group organizations such as CHADD, ADDIEN, and ADDA.

NOTES

1. Fulghum, R. (1986). *All I really need to know I learned in kindergarten.* New York: Ivy Books. Back cover.

Chapter 2

The Mystery of
the Missing Social Skills

REBECCA WAS ANXIOUS to make a good impression in her first meeting with the board of directors of her new company. She had not done well in her previous job, though she wasn't exactly sure what had gone wrong. As long as she could remember, she had always had difficulty with people. She liked them, but they often seemed unfriendly to her. But this time, she felt, things would be different. It was great to have a fresh start.

Completely absorbed in planning what she'd say and do, Rebecca lost track of time. Though she had planned to arrive ten minutes early, she suddenly found herself ten minutes late. Quickly gathering up her scattered materials, she ran to the meeting, getting there late, out of breath, and looking a little disheveled. In her haste, she had forgotten to put on her suit jacket or comb her hair.

Rushing into the room, Rebecca sat in the first available chair she saw, which was at the table with the board members. She did not notice that all the other staff members were sitting on the outskirts of the room. This table was apparently reserved for the board—she was the only staff member

19

sitting there—but in her haste, she had missed that unwritten rule.

As the meeting proceeded, Rebecca interrupted the speakers on numerous occasions. She wasn't trying to be rude; she just knew she'd forget what she wanted to say if she had to wait. She did not notice the annoyance on the faces of the others at the table. When it came time to present her project, she realized that she had left her presentation materials in her office. She tried to improvise without the visual aids she had worked on all week, but it didn't go very well.

Even though she had spent a great deal of time on the project and had wonderful ideas, the others were blinded by her apparent incompetence so they dismissed her ideas. They began looking down as she spoke, turning away from her. Then came the subtle comments—"Thank you, Rebecca, we'll keep this in mind." "That's certainly one way to see it. Are there others?" But Rebecca didn't pick up on their facial expressions and verbal prompts. Absorbed in her project, she continued to tell them about her ideas. They wanted her to stop talking, but she wasn't getting it. Their indirect message was becoming more and more direct as she went on. Finally, a board member said in a rather loud, gruff voice, "Would you please shut up and sit down!"

Rebecca felt crushed and blind-sided. Why are people always so mean to me? she wondered. Everyone is always rejecting me and my ideas. She had hoped this job would be different, but it happened again. Why? She had no clue.

What They Don't Teach You in School

You may have guessed by now that Rebecca has AD/HD. People with AD/HD often have to read everything a second or third time, to try to pick up what they missed in the first reading. You may have developed tricks to remember things. You write things down. People with AD/HD can be brilliantly creative and dazzlingly enjoyable because their minds are always moving. However, you also lack the mental filters needed to stay on one subject. You must work extra hard to rein in your galloping thoughts.

Rebecca was already quite an achiever to win this job in the first place. Her impressive credentials were evidence of her ability. Despite her AD/HD, she had gotten through school and into the workplace, in positions of responsibility at several different companies. That's why it's sadly ironic that this painful episode in the boardroom wasn't caused by a reading problem or a failure to focus—it was her violation of a number of unwritten social rules. Quite simply, she lacked social skills.

What does that have to do with AD/HD? Everything. It was Rebecca's struggle with AD/HD that prevented her from noticing what others often take for granted. She had learned to read *words* as a child, after considerable effort, but she had never learned to read *people*. Because of her inability to recognize subtle cues, she behaved inappropriately among the very people she was trying to impress.

You may have the same struggle. You may have won the battle of academic learning and professional accomplishment, but you're still having trouble with the basic do's and don'ts of social interaction. After your tremendous effort to overcome the other obstacles of AD/HD, this can be extremely discouraging.

Social skills are not officially taught in school, yet they're expected and often required of us all. Punishments are harsh for those who violate these social expectations. People who lack social skills often end up like Rebecca—dismissed, rejected, but never knowing what they did wrong. Everyone is expected to just *have* these basic social skills so no one really talks much about them. Therefore, people who lack these skills have a hard time learning from their mistakes. Rebecca has no clue about her social gaffes, and she'll probably never be told. So without help, she's likely to repeat the same mistakes over and over again.

What are Social Skills?

Social skills are all the things we should say and do (and shouldn't say and do) when we interact with other people. One expert calls them "specific abilities that enable a person to perform competently at particular social tasks."[1] A team of researchers offers another definition:

> A social skill is any cognitive function or overt behavior in which an individual engages while interacting with another person or persons. Cognitive functions include such capacities as empathizing with or understanding another person's feelings, discriminating and evaluating consequences for social behavior. Overt behaviors include the nonverbal (e.g., head nods, eye contact, facial expression) and verbal (e.g., what the persons says) components of a social performance. [2]

Social skills are generally acquired through incidental learning: watching people, copying the behavior of others, practicing, and getting feedback. Most people start this process in kindergarten or earlier. As children become aware of the world around them, they observe, copy, practice, and learn from feedback. Much of their "playing grown-up" involves the practicing and honing of these social skills. Watch children in their role playing and you'll see the most basic of social interactions: "Hello, Mr. Jones." "Hello, Mrs. Smith." "How are you?" "I'm fine." It seems so simple, but there's an intricate learning process at work.

But children with AD/HD often miss those details. So they never go through this process of observing, copying, practicing, and getting feedback. As an adult you may have picked up pieces of the pattern through the years, learning the hard way, but you're still missing other pieces. And the worst thing is, you may not know what you're missing.

Police storm into a house in search of a missing man. Relatives haven't heard from this elderly uncle, and they fear foul play. But there's no sign of him in the house. They call out, but there's no answer, just the hum of a refrigerator and random tapping of branches against the roof. The police turn to go, but one detective stops.

"Wait," he says. "Those aren't trees tapping. That's Morse Code." An old Navy man, he recognizes that telegraph language and quickly decodes the tapping as a cry for help. They rush upstairs and find the missing man, who had fallen in his attic and now was too weak to call out for help.

The story may be a bit dramatic, but it illustrates social skills. The tapping was there all the time, but no one recognized it, except the one detective who knew the code. In the same way, there are social cues used all around us, but folks with AD/HD tend to miss them because you don't know the code. Sometimes it must feel as if everyone else has read some instruction book and you haven't; and you're always breaking rules you don't even know exist. That's not far from the truth. Others have learned the code of social skills and somehow you missed it. They *are* seeing and hearing things that you don't. Well, you see and hear the same cues, but you don't recognize them as cues, just like those other policemen who thought they just heard branches tapping on the roof.

Social skills aren't invisible. They're comprised of specific verbal and nonverbal behaviors that can be observed—once you know what you're looking for. They involve back-and-forth behavior, the subtle signals people give each other to show interest or lack of it, encouragement, hostility, agreement, romance, or status. Certain signals call for certain responses. If you don't respond appropriately, a conversation can come to a grinding halt—or your companion may just think you're a bit weird.

To make matters more complex, different situations often require different social skills. A boardroom is different from a football stadium. You don't want to start "the wave" during a stockholders report. If you're learning social skills, you don't just have to know what they are, but you also must learn which responses to use in which settings. If you behave the wrong way in the wrong place, you'll get strange looks. The good news is that you can learn the code. You can develop social skills.

What People Think of You—and Why

People are constantly trying to make sense of the world around them by questioning situations. *Why did this happen? Why did he say that? Why didn't she arrive on time? Why does he always forget to call?*

The process of establishing a causal relationship—answering the question, "why"—is complex. People don't usually have all the information needed to fully understand a situation, but that doesn't stop them from trying to make sense of it anyway. Since people don't have all the facts, they make guesses based on the things that they can see (external cues) and things they already know. Unfortunately, many treat those guesses with a great deal of certainty. "I don't know for sure, but *it must be because . . .*" People don't like maybes, so they work hard to find suitable explanations for what happens. This process of trying to understand the causes of social events and behavior is called ***attribution theory***. [3]

The process of attribution theory is similar to a detective gathering clues while trying to solve a mystery. Based on pieces of information, people begin to put together their understanding of the *why*. Once enough pieces are in place, a causal attribution is made.

John is late today. In fact, John has been late for as long as I've known him. It's really getting to be a problem. I guess (this is attribution theory!) John is always late because he doesn't value our relationship. I just know that's the problem!

Attributions are not always accurate. In an effort to try to understand and find the *why*, people may jump to conclusions. As a result of their attribution errors, many people become angry, frustrated, or annoyed at friends and family with AD/HD. They have decided that the behavior was intentional. This happens so much that the social psychologists even named this mistake. It's called the *fundamental attribution error.* [4] People also tend to have their explanation rely too much on a person's internal characteristics (mean, bad, lazy, etc.) and too little on external factors (AD/HD, no sleep the night before, sickness, etc.). This fundamental attribution error is why so many of you get blamed. In their search for understanding, others are likely to assume that something must be wrong with you. Attribution theory is important for you to know about when you have AD/HD, because people around you regularly misinterpret your actions.

The title of a popular book on adult AD/HD, *You Mean I'm Not Lazy, Stupid or Craxy?!* by Kate Kelly and Peggy Ramundo[4], illustrates some of the negative attributes generally given to those with AD/HD.

- When you take too long on a project because your mind is drifting, people think you're being lazy. They assume that you could apply yourself if you wanted to, so they attribute your slow pace to laziness.

- When you blurt out ideas because the impulse hits you, or when you move erratically because of your hyperactivity, people may attribute your behavior to craziness. Because they can't see any purpose to your words or actions, they assume there is none.

- When you have to read the same page four times because of the "blinks and blanks" in your attention, people think you're stupid and can't understand the words or ideas. Because they get it on the first reading, they assume that any intelligent person could. Since it doesn't come quickly to you, they attribute this to stupidity.

It's an incredible relief to many people with AD/HD when they're finally diagnosed. Suddenly they have an explanation for their own behaviors. The Kelly-Ramundo title(*You Mean I'm Not Lazy, Stupid, or Crazy?!*) captures that feeling of reassurance. No, you're not lazy, stupid, or crazy. Chances are, you're quite intelligent, rational, and hard-working. You just have this problem called AD/HD.

It's important to understand why people are reaching the conclusions they are reaching. Their conclusions or attributions often shine a negative light on you. However, you can help people change their attributions, which will cast a more favorable light on you and your behavior.

Attributions basically serve two purposes:

1. To help determine feelings and attitudes about people or events.
2. To help people predict and control their environment.

Attributions help determine feelings and attitudes about people or events. It's often the *interpretation* of an event or action that triggers emotional reactions, rather than the actual event or action itself. Our feelings, attitudes, and behavior toward others are determined by our *ideas* about their motives.

Karen stewed as she waited for her friend Terri in the lobby of the restaurant. They had planned to meet for dinner at 6:30 that night, but Terri was late. At first, Karen assumed traffic was bad, or maybe Terri had received a phone call as she headed out the door, or maybe Terri had to work late. She struggled to find a reason why her friend was a half-hour late. Terri couldn't have forgotten; they had confirmed it earlier that day.

When Karen called, she got Terri's machine. Obviously Terri was out somewhere, but not at the restaurant where she was supposed to be. As she thought more about it, Karen figured Terri must have gotten a "better" offer from someone else. Maybe some guy had called. Or maybe she went shopping, forgetting about her dinner with Karen.

After an hour, Karen drove back home, still trying to account for her friend's absence. How dare she stand me up like this! She can't call herself my friend and treat me this way! I'll give her a piece of my mind. As she opened her front door, the phone was ringing. It was Terri.

"I'm so sorry about dinner," she began, "but just as I was leaving, I got a call."

"I knew it," thought Karen, her anger intensifying.

"It was my mom, calling from the hospital. My dad had a heart attack. She was really a basket case. I had to get over there right away. This is the first chance I've had to call you."

Instantly Karen's anger fizzled. Terri had an explanation—a why—and a good one. Of course she had to rush to the hospital! It was her dad! Her mom needed comfort! Karen would have done the same thing.

According to attribution theory, Karen needed to find a reason for Terri's behavior. That is, she had to explain why Terri didn't show up. She assumed that Terri just didn't care about their dinner, and Karen was responding with anger. But here's the important thing: What made Karen angry? Waiting at the restaurant? Not really, because after she knew the whole story, she wasn't mad anymore. She was angry because she thought Terri didn't care. That thought upset her— even though the thought turned out to be wrong.

Similarly, a friend might be offended if you forgot his or her birthday. Birthdays are important, and if the day passes without any recognition from a friend, it may seem as if that person doesn't care. People might attribute an uncaring feeling to that person as a way of explaining the action (or in this case, non-action) of forgetting the birthday. But if they knew you had AD/HD and generally had difficulty with dates, even important dates, there'd be another explanation. They could attribute the act of forgetting to AD/HD, and not take it personally.

Here's an idea of how attribution theory works in the life of those with AD/HD who are trying to navigate social relationships:

What you do	The attribution	What it really means
You are late.	You don't care. You are selfish.	You have AD/HD. It is difficult to be on time, but you do care.
You forget to pick up your child from football practice.	You are a bad, thoughtless parent.	You have AD/HD. Sometimes you forget important things. You love your child.
You buy a new car without consulting your spouse.	You don't value his/her input. You are selfish.	You have AD/HD. and act impulsively. You struggle with money management.

Attributions help people predict and control their environment.

When people understand the reason for an action, they can begin to feel that they have some sense of control. A lack of understanding usually causes a great deal of anxiety. People become upset and worried if the world doesn't make sense. That's why a random, senseless act of aggression, like a school bombing, causes so much distress. Along with the great sadness, there is also great apprehension. Why did this happen? How can we make sure it doesn't happen again?

Finding the *why* is especially important in our social interactions, because we expect people to act a certain way in different situations. There's safety in knowing what someone will do or what will generally happen. We can better anticipate how people will act and that makes us more comfortable with them.

People need this consistency in the world and in the behavior of the people around them. When a person does something unexpected, inappropriate, or seemingly out of character, there's a struggle to explain it. When others break those expectations, people respond first with excuses and simple explanations—the "bad day" approach. Sometimes people are excused, especially if they have a track record of good behavior. "He's under a lot of stress right now." "She's having a bad day." Their behavior makes sense. The world is still predictable.

But when the actions are repeated or intensified, the easy answers don't work anymore. Then people start to attribute negative motives to those who are acting inappropriately. They are no longer able to control their world and they don't like that feeling. This gives people a reason to feel negatively toward the offenders.

Many feel uncomfortable when their life is disorganized. You may often hear, "I need to know what you will do so that I won't be caught off guard." In the fluctuating world of AD/HD, people's needs to predict and control can be difficult for you to accommodate. The world of those with AD/HD rarely fits neatly into a structured, controllable, predictable box! These fluctuations can be difficult for others to accept as they try to structure and control their world.

But you may have found that people's attitudes change when they learn about your AD/HD. They seem nicer to you, don't they? They may still be frustrated with you, but not as angry. What's happening? Suddenly they have something else to which they can attribute your behavior. It's not that you're uncaring, selfish, or controlling—it's the AD/HD. They may still become frustrated with your behavior at times, but at least they know you're not *intentionally trying* to bother them. Hopefully others will understand your social violation through the framework of AD/HD. As a result, they should feel better about their social interactions with you!

The Catch

Now you know that there are problems with the attributions people tend to make. First, they figure that everyone is in complete control of their minds and bodies, completely ignoring the impulsivity, hyperactivity, and attention surges associated with AD/HD. But they also assume that "everybody knows" the unwritten rules of social interaction.

That's a problem for many of you who never learned these rules. Those social rules remain mysterious precisely because they're unwritten. No one teaches these things to adults, and people rarely even tell you when you've violated a social rule—they just roll their eyes or snicker behind your back. Locked into their assumptions that "everybody" knows how to act in social settings, they often think the worst of people who don't.

We began this chapter with the story of Rebecca's meeting. In her meeting, Rebecca came across as a self-absorbed loudmouth when she was really quite insecure. Just as she misunderstood the signals of the people in that boardroom, they misunderstood her and her intentions.

There are many lonely people who suffer only because they never learned how to use basic social skills. Social blunders alienate others and adults with AD/HD seem to suffer more in the area of social rejection and feelings of isolation than the general population.

Through hard work and discipline, you can compensate for many of the drawbacks of AD/HD, but a lack of social skills can still set you apart. I've seen this in two people who are very close to me. My father (who has AD/HD) has always only had a few friends, due in large part to his numerous social violations. My son, Jarryd, has been very frustrated by the rules he constantly is breaking and the social rejection that follows. He asks a simple question: "Why don't they just tell me?"

Why Don't They Just Tell Me?

Many with AD/HD ask the same question. Why are social skills so mysterious? Why aren't people better at coaching those who are having a hard time with the basics? My son's playmates would be quick to teach him how to swing a baseball bat, but when it comes to general rules of conversation, they're silent. "I can't believe that they won't play with me because I talk too much sometimes," Jarryd complains. "All they have to do is tell me to shut up." And I'll shut up. But if I don't know that I'm talking too much, how can I know when it's time to be quiet?"

Apparently that's one of those unwritten rules: *Don't correct someone for being rude.* They hint, they complain to others, sometimes they're rude in response—but only the most outspoken people (or the most caring) will tell you directly when you're breaking the social rules. They're afraid to hurt your feelings. They don't want to act like ogres, social cops, know-it-alls, or nags. After all, they figure, you already know how to behave. Everybody does. Right?

They're wrong. In fact, people sometimes use an interesting word sometimes to describe behavior that breaks the social rules. "That person is so *ignorant!*" The word, of course, means "not knowing." It perfectly describes the situation of many with AD/HD who just don't know the rules. But when people call someone ignorant, there is a negative implication. They assume the "ignorant" person just doesn't *want* to know or just doesn't care about others. They don't realize that some so-called "ignorant" people care very much, but they're truly "not knowing." In fact, they're desperate to learn the rules that everyone else lives by—if only someone would teach them.

Social acceptance can be viewed as a spiral going up or down. If you have good social skills, you win acceptance from those around you, which gives you the feedback you need to develop better social skills.

Sadly, for those with AD/HD, the spiral often goes the other way. Their lack of social skills leads to peer rejection, which then limits opportunities to learn social skills, which leads to more rejection, and so on. You can't learn the rules of the game unless you play, you can't play if others aren't playing with you, and they won't play with you if you don't know the rules. What a vicious cycle!

I hope that this book will break that downward spiral by teaching you the social skills you need in order to gain acceptance. Then you can reverse the spiral, learning more and more social skills from the people with whom you're spending time.

Social skills can be best understood by dividing them into different types: manners, communication skills, reading the situation, and interpersonal skills. And there is a chapter devoted to each one. These skills are really not all that mysterious, once you know what to look for. The rest of this book, will address the unique social challenges of AD/HD and then help you to develop a plan to learn or improve the social skills you'll need most.

Learn to understand the subtle cues that others give you. Some people will help you if you ask them to, and I hope this book will give you a nudge in the right direction.

JUST THE FACTS

- Many adults with AD/HD fear they will never fit in, no matter how hard they try because of social skill difficulties.

- Social skills are all the things we should say and do (and shouldn't say and do) when we interact with other people.

- It's hard to learn social skills later in life because everybody assumes you already know them. AD/HD may prevent you from noticing the social skills that others often take for granted.

- Social skills aren't invisible. They're made up of specific, observable verbal and nonverbal behaviors—once you know what you're looking for.

- This process of trying to understand why people do what they do is called *attribution theory*.

- Unfortunately, attributions are not always accurate. Others are likely to attribute your behavior to something that must be wrong with *you* rather than understanding the behavior as part of AD/HD.

- If you help others understand AD/HD, this can change.

NOTES

1. McFall, R.M. (1982). A review and reformulation of the concept of social skills. *Behavioral Assessment, 4,* 1-33. Cited in *Assessment and instruction of social skills,* L. Elksnin & N. Elksnin (1995). San Diego: Singular Publishing Group, Inc., p.4.

2. Schumaker, J.B., & Hazel, J.S. (1984). Social Skills assessment and training for the learning disabled: Who's on first and what's on second? Part 1. *Journal of Learning Disabilities, 17,* 422-431. Cited in *Assessment and instruction of social skills,* L. Elksnin & N. Elksnin (1995). San Diego: Singular Publishing Group, Inc., p.4.

3. Taylor, S., Peplau, L., & Sears, D. (1997). *Social psychology (9th ed.).* New Jersey: Prentice Hall, p. 55.

4. Kelly, K. & Ramundo, P. (1996). *You mean I'm not lazy, stupid or crazy?!* New York: Fireside.

Part Two

What Does AD/HD Have to Do with Social Skills?

Chapter 3

Can't Everyone Fry an Egg, Read the Paper, Watch TV, and Listen to Someone Talk at the Same Time?: Inattention

JARRYD WAS IN the family room and he wanted to talk. He'd had a tough day at school and was telling me about his problems. I, however, was having a difficult time listening because he was standing up, swinging a tennis racket, kicking his legs, and watching TV while he was talking with me. I asked Jarryd to put the tennis racket down and look at me while he was talking. I had coached him before on "active listening." This is a counseling technique where you sit facing the person you are talking with and look at the person, maintaining good eye contact. So I asked him to do "active listening." Jarryd responded, "But mom, I am being active while I'm listening." We both laughed at his play on words.

But it's important to note in this story that Jarryd was not the one having difficulty listening. I—the person without AD/HD—was having a difficult time listening to him because of all of his movement and the appearance of inattention.

Good relationships are built on good communication. The ability to communicate effectively with other people is readily recognized as a necessary social skill. But effective communication means *paying attention* to someone, and that can be a problem for those with AD/HD.

In fact, when adults with AD/HD tell about their interpersonal difficulties, many of these difficulties stem from inattention. That's not surprising, of course. We are talking about *Attention Deficit/Hyperactive Disorder* (AD/HD).

Difficulties with inattention seem to fall into two basic categories. The first category involves listening but not looking like you're listening. The second category involves thinking that you're listening but failing to comprehend all that is said.

Listening but not looking like you are

You never listen to me!

How many times have you heard that? You may be hanging on every word, but if it *looks* like your mind is elsewhere, people will assume you're not listening. And based on what we know about attribution theory, they will also think that you don't care about them. Or they may think you're rude. Or they may think that you find them boring. Any of these thoughts can create bad feelings between you and the speakers—even if they're not true.

I've counseled many couples with this problem. Their dialogue usually sounds something like this:

Donna:	*You never listen to me.*
Jim:	*I do, too!*
Donna:	*You do not!*
Jim:	*I do, too! I heard everything you said.*
Donna:	*So what did I just say?*

40

| Jim: | *You said . . . (and he triumphantly repeats what she said).* |
| Donna: | *Lucky guess!* |

She's still frustrated, and he feels falsely accused.

In our society, listening means much more than merely being able to repeat words. In the counseling field a great deal of time and effort goes into teaching future therapists to "actively listen" to their clients.[1] In fact, the very first communication skill counselors learn is *looking* attentive. Most clients would not be happy if their therapist was listening to them while writing a report, listening to the radio, and looking out the window—even if that therapist could repeat every word they said! The same principles hold true in everyday conversation. Effective communication is much more than mere words or the simple exchange of information. In a relationship, people don't just want to be heard when they talk. They want to be *understood*. Effective communication involves letting the person know that you care about what they are saying and that you're trying to understand.

Looking attentive does the trick. When you listen actively, people feel that you understand them, or at least are trying to understand them. And that sense of understanding helps build relationships. Chapter 8 is full of ideas to help you improve your skills in this area.

EXERCISE

Active Listening

Try out this "active listening" position perhaps in front of a mirror or with a willing partner:

1. Sit facing another person (or a pretend person)

41

> 2. Open posture (uncrossed arms, hands, legs and feet)
> 3. Lean slightly forward
> 4. Maintain appropriate eye contact

It's ironic that this basic communication skill isn't about talking better or hearing more accurately. It's just looking like you're listening. The ability to look attentive is a very important social skill for you to acquire. In my story at the beginning of the chapter, Jarryd wasn't having difficulty following our conversation—I was. He was able to engage in multiple tasks at the same time. I was not. Because he lacked certain active listening skills, I did not feel that we were communicating effectively.

So why is that his problem? Shouldn't I just trust that he's paying attention even though he's looking elsewhere? Well, I try to, but I'm his mother. Other people won't be as patient. If he wants to make and keep friends, he has to learn to look like he's paying attention.

Remember that communication is more than talking and hearing. In a conversation, you are sending messages with everything you *do*, as well as what you say. If you say something and I roll my eyes, I'm sending a message that I don't buy what you're saying. If I say something and you're turned away, watching TV, you're sending the message that you don't care about what I'm saying—even if you do. It's hard for someone to keep conversing with you under those circumstances.

It might help to think of undivided attention as a gift. You might be able to pay attention to a lot of different things at the same time, and people ought to know that about you. But if you care about someone, you want to send the message,

"What you say is important to me." You want to focus your full attention on them.

Many people with AD/HD find it incredibly difficult to focus on only one thing at a time. Many find it painfully slow and boring to just sit and listen to someone talk while ideas and sounds are dancing in their heads. That's why you have to decide to give this as a gift. It's an *expensive* gift, too, but it will be worth it.

If you don't have AD/HD, but regularly interact with someone who does, you need to recognize and appreciate the effort involved in giving the gift of attention. For those without AD/HD, listening requires minimal effort. (In fact, those of us without AD/HD have even been accused of having an Attention *Surplus* Disorder!) But attention is expensive for those with AD/HD, and can't be taken for granted.

ACTIVE LISTENING
TIPS FOR THOSE WITHOUT AD/HD

- Ask specifically for "active listening" (or use another code word) at the beginning of an especially important conversation.
- Plan important conversations in an area that promotes the ability to focus. Avoid distracting surroundings.
- Since active listening requires effort, keep conversations brief and to the point.
- Thank the person with AD/HD for giving you the gift of attention.

You think you're listening but fail to hear all that's said

Sandra arrived early at work, ready to begin that special project that was due in a week. She proudly put the papers in order and began working at the computer. Focusing on the project, she quickly completed the first three sections. This time she would not be late. This time she would be successful. She went into the hall to take a break. But the hall was filled with people talking and the sounds of business machines in action. There she met her boss who was hurrying off to a meeting. He asked her about her progress on the project. Sandra proudly told him that she was well on target for the completion date next week. He was pleased and told her so.

Basking in the praise, she failed to hear his next words: "Give me a progress report at the end of the day to take to the board meeting tonight." He again wished her well and she went back to work on the project. Sandra worked tirelessly on the project, beaming from the encouragement of her boss. The project was coming together nicely. Sandra went home very pleased with herself.

But there was no progress report on the boss's desk at the end of the day!

The next day the boss was very angry with Sandra's lack of follow-through on such an important matter. Since this was not the first time Sandra had failed to follow instructions, he put her on probation. Sandra was heartbroken and confused. She thought she had done all that was asked of her. "Why are people so difficult to work with?" she wondered.

The diagnosis of AD/HD does not mean that you have an absence of attention, but rather that you have an *inconsistent attentional pattern*[2]. At times—in fact, most times—conversations are heard. But sometimes there are lapses in attention because you have shifted focus. Often this shift of focus goes unnoticed by both parties in a conversation, and that can cause problems. We saw that in Sandra's story, she never knew she missed her boss's instructions, and neither did he.

Jim Reisinger, president of ADDien (Adult Attention Deficit Disorder Information Exchange), describes these brief lapses of attention as "blinks" [3] For those with AD/HD, he says, the world is sprinkled with information holes created by these blinks. Since no one realizes that a blink has occurred, everyone *assumes* that everyone heard all the information that was said. And we all know what happens when you assume something!

Marie:	*I'm going to the store. Do you want anything?*
Dave:	*Yes, I need some more milk and cereal.*
Marie:	*No problem.*
Dave:	*Thanks! (And now Marie blinks.) Oh, and while you are going that way please pick up Jason from soccer practice.*
Marie:	*All right, I'll see you later.*

After a little while, Marie returns with her groceries, and the milk and cereal that Dave had requested.

Dave:	*Where's Jason?*
Marie:	*I don't know. You were supposed to get him.*
Dave:	*But I thought you were going to get him on your way back from the store.*
Marie:	*We never even talked about that.*
Dave:	*We did too!*

45

> *Marie:*   *We did not! You're always making up things we never even discuss!*
>
> *Dave:*   *You're just irresponsible. You never do what you are supposed to do!*

As you can see, a little ill-timed blink can quickly become the fuel for some rather huge interpersonal difficulties. Inattention is frequently attributed to such defects in character as irresponsibility, laziness, or defiance. Without understanding that attentional difficulties are a part of AD/HD, and not character flaws, there can be many misunderstandings, and hurt feelings.

Sometimes you may get into the habit of covering up your difficulty with attention by just saying *OK*. Because it can be embarrassing to constantly miss pieces of conversation, some are reluctant to ask others to repeat the missed information. But this *OK* habit can create big problems. Even though it may provide a short-term break and get you off the hook, you'll pay the price later when you find out what exactly you unknowingly agreed to with your *OK*.

For Those Who Blink

If you sometimes blink, you'll find the following communication skills helpful:

1. Realize that perhaps you don't always hear everything that's said.
2. Check out what you heard to make sure you got the complete message.

Realize that perhaps you don't always hear everything that's said. This first skill is really an attitude shift. Accept that you may need repetition.

46

Check out what you heard to make sure you got the complete message. The second is a skill you need to practice. Luckily, this is a quick one! In most cases it will take less than a minute to repeat what you just heard. But this habit will go a long way toward improving your social skills and saving you from costly misunderstandings.

What if our stories had turned out like this?

Story #1

Sandra: *I'm glad you're happy with my progress on the project. I'll be sure you have it by next week. Was there anything else?*

Boss: *Don't forget to give me a copy of the report by the end of the day for me to take to the board meeting.*

Sandra: *Okay, end of the day. No problem.*

Story #2

Marie: *I'm leaving now and I'll get your milk and cereal. Was there anything else?*

Dave: *Yes, don't forget to pick up Jason from soccer practice.*

Marie: *Okay, I'll pick up Jason on my way home. See you later.*

In both cases, the very act of repeating what was heard and asking for clarification would have prevented the difficulties by "filling in the blink."

EXERCISE

Filling in the Blink

1. Try repeating what you have heard.
2. Ask if there was anything you left out.
3. See if you can "fill in the blinks" before interpersonal difficulties erupt.

FILLING IN THE BLINKS
TIPS FOR THOSE WITHOUT AD/HD

1. Ask the person with AD/HD to repeat any directions or instructions you have given to make sure that all theinformation was heard correctly.

2. Clarify or fill in gaps as needed.

JUST THE FACTS

- The ability to communicate effectively with others is a basic social skill.
- Inattention is the primary characteristic of AD/HD and attentional difficulties are at the center of many interpersonal difficulties for those with AD/HD.

Difficulty #1:

Listening but not looking like you are listening.

Work on "active listening":

Give the *gift* of your complete attention even though it is *expensive* to give.

48

Difficulty #2:

Thinking that you are listening but failing to hear all that is said.

Information holes created by "blinks" or brief periods of inattention go unnoticed. People often *assume* that everyone heard everything that was said. Interpersonal conflict often results if something important was lost in the blink.

Work on:

- Repeating what you heard.
- Asking if you left out anything.
- Fill in the blinks before interpersonal difficulties erupt.

NOTES

1. Egan, G. (1998). *The skilled helper: A problem management approach to helping* (6th ed.). Pacific Grove, California: Brooks Cole Publishing Company.
2. Barkley, R. (1997). *ADHD and the nature of self-control.* New York: Guilford Press.
3. Reisinger, J. (1997). *BLINKS: A phenomenon of distractibility in attention deficit disorder*, PO Box 1701, Ann Arbor, MI 48106.

Chapter 4

Ready, Fire, Aim: Impulsivity

THE MOVIE, *MRS. DOUBTFIRE,* starring Robin Williams, is a comedy, but a closer look at the film reveals something more serious—the difficulties that result when a person acts impulsively. Now I don't want to start diagnosing fictional characters, but the impulsive actions of Williams's character early in the film are pretty consistent with AD/HD.

First, he fights with his boss and quits his job. Not the wisest thing to do. He's acting impulsively, following his emotions and failing to consider the consequences of his actions. Then, without any planning, he decides to throw a lavish birthday party for his son. Of course his wife, knowing nothing about it, comes home to find a petting zoo in the house. She's had enough. She asks for a divorce.[1]

Adults with AD/HD often have difficulty thinking before they act.

Their motto: *Ready, Fire, Aim.* [2]

51

You may know the rules and even be able to explain them, but you can't always *follow* them. This inability to control your actions is known as *impulsivity*—one of the hallmarks of AD/HD behavior. "They know what to do but don't do what they know. They have difficulty weighing the consequences of their actions before acting and do not reasonably consider the consequences of their past behavior." [3]

A college student was telling me about his fraternity's wonderful idea about how to deal with the winter blahs. They live in Maine where it snows much of the winter (sometimes even fall and spring), and they thought it would be fun to have a beach party in their basement during the winter. They had a truck deliver a couple hundred tons of sand by shooting the sand through a living room window through a hole they had strategically placed in the living room floor. The plan worked. The basement was filled with sand and transformed into a beach. They had a great beach party complete with beach blankets, beach umbrellas, beach music, and girls in bikinis.

*It was only after the party that they realized they had failed to consider the consequences of their action. How do you get a couple hundred tons of sand **out** of the basement?*

It's not exactly that people with AD/HD don't learn from past experiences. You learn but it's hard for you to act differently based on your new knowledge. Often you may understand the situation, but your need for immediate gratification outweighs the limits of your self-control. "I want it *now*." You know a hundred reasons not to do what you're doing, but in that moment, it doesn't matter. As a result, you're often repeat offenders, which causes great frustration to those around you.[4]

When Jarryd was a toddler, he loved to color. Unfortunately he had a hard time restricting his coloring to paper. Though I kept reminding him not to use his crayons on other household things, he kept doing this. One morning I came downstairs and found Jarryd in his sleeper pj's, crayon in hand, coloring circles on our family room wall. As he was coloring the circles he was repeating, "No, no color on walls. No, no color on walls." He knew that he should not be coloring on the wall. He was even repeating the rule. He even seemed to be trying not to color on the wall. But the impulse was too strong. Too tempting. He was coloring on the wall.

I have worked with many adults with AD/HD who struggled with impulsivity. No, they weren't coloring on walls, but they were often doing things they knew they shouldn't. Yet they seemed to lack the self-control that was necessary to change their behavior.

Jeff was coming to counseling for the first time for assessment of AD/HD. The secretary greeted him, asked him to have a seat in the waiting room and informed him that the counselor would be with him soon. He had an appointment for 10:00 and it was 9:45. Jeff sat and waited. He waited for about a minute. He then jumped up, knocked on the counselor's closed door with the "Do not disturb" sign, opened the door, and said, "I just wanted to let you know that I am here." He was told by the startled counselor to please wait outside until the session in progress was finished. Jeff sat down once again and waited. He waited about two minutes. He again jumped up, knocked on the closed door with the "Do not disturb" sign, opened the door and said, "I just wanted to let you know that I have a hard time waiting!" He could tell that the counselor and client were getting angry with his interruptions. "I know, I'll just wait out here. I'm sorry."

"I know. I'm sorry."

That could be the catchphrase for AD/HD impulsivity. Most people assume that mistakes come from ignorance— once you know the rules, of course you'll follow them. But it's not always so with AD/HD. Often the rules are known, but the impulse is too strong. It's also assumed (attribution theory strikes again), if you do not follow the rules that you know, that you must be rude, arrogant, or self-centered. Not a great image to promote social status.

For those who deal with impulsive people, life can be a constant roller coaster with fast and furious ups and downs. At least it's never boring. Jerry Mills, an adult with AD/HD, wrote a song that describes the struggle of many impulsive adults with AD/HD.

Impulse

by Jerry Mills

Well, I wake up every morning. I've got my best laid plans all made.
But before I ever hit full stride my mind has strayed.

*And like a pinball on the ricochet, I bounce
around my life.*
*But usually end up home again in my bed at
night.*

My life's an impulse!
So don't ask me what my life's about
*'Cuz life is certainly one thing I can't figure
out.*
*So I figured I'd stop to rest awhile but I won't
be stopping long,*
*'Cuz I'll be catching another impulse and like
. . . that I'm gone!*

Now I never wanted to be this way
It's just the way my brain is wired.
*And don't think, because I'm happy now, that
I don't get tired.*
*Of never ever knowing where I'm goin', how
far or how long.*
*But I usually end up at home at night with
another song.*

My life's an impulse!
And in a heartbeat I can change my mind.
*And head off on some whim to see what I can
find.*
So I figured I'd rest my brain awhile,
But instead I wrote this song
*About catching another impulse and like . . .
that I'm gone!*

My life's an impulse!
We need more impulse to get us movin' again.
And one day we'll all look back here to where
we've been.
And it'll blow our minds the day we find
That we've moved light years straight ahead.
And all because we followed where our . . .
impulse led.

My life's an impulse!
So don't ask me what my life's about,
'Cuz life is certainly one thing I can't figure
out.
So I figured I'd stop to rest awhile but I won't
be stopping long,
'Cuz I'll be catchin' another impulse and like
. . . that I'm gone![5]

Impulse was reprinted with permission. © 1993 Jerry Mills/ASCAP

Although this bouncing around is often exciting for you, it's often difficult for those without AD/HD to share in the excitement of the moment. You may overwhelm those who are more linear and orderly.

"Hey. I have a great idea! Let's take a trip next week instead of staying home."

"That has possibilities. What were you thinking about?"

"I think we should pack up and go cross country for ten days. It would be great! We can see all sorts of things that we have been talking about. We can . . ."

"Hold on just a minute. That sounds nice, but let's look at reality. You're always coming up with these pie-in-the-sky

ideas. I'm always the one who has to figure out how to do it. Do you have any idea of what's involved in planning a trip like this? And you want to leave in three days? Do you . . ."

"You are such a party pooper. You're not much fun. You always shoot down my ideas. Why can't you for just once say, that's a great idea, let's go for it? No. It's always about planning. Planning is so boring. By the time you do all that planning you never get a chance to do anything. Sorry I even bothered you. Let's just stay home." (Door slam)

Others become overwhelmed as they try to plan out sequentially the ideas that dance through the impulsive person's mind. While the *idea* of going cross-country may sound thrilling, the *actuality* of such a trip can be quite detailed. There are maps to be studied, reservations to be made, plans for taking care of home for a period of time (mail, pets, plants, etc.). You probably don't think of all those details.

And yet, if it weren't for the impulsive ideas, life could be rather boring for the linear thinkers. Wild ideas can create joy and adventure. Sure, linear thinkers need to make careful plans, but if there are no impulsive ideas, what plans are there to make? Many great leaders—entrepreneurs in business and innovators in the arts—are considered impulsive. They rely on impulsivity to move forward when others try to hold them back. So you don't want to get rid of your impulses, just make sure they don't get you in too much trouble.

Let's consider some of these areas of difficulty one by one.

Interrupting Someone Who's Speaking

You may have a difficult time holding your thoughts during a conversation. When the other person says something that sparks a thought in your head, you might jump right in with a response. Polite conversation requires that you wait for the other person to stop or pause. But you may interrupt in mid-sentence, because you're thinking, "If I don't say what I'm thinking, it will be gone. I must say it now!"

In some high-energy conversations, that's fine. The other person may interrupt you right back. But usually an interruption is considered to be an insult to the person speaking.

> *Obviously you're more interested in your own thoughts than in mine.*
>
> *You must not care what I have to say, because you don't let me talk.*
>
> *You must not value me.*

That's how the interrupted person often feels. And that will hurt your relationship with that person. He or she won't want to *talk* with you if you keep interrupting. And more importantly, he or she won't want to be with you.

Impulsively Entering a Group and Interrupting

Imagine that you see a group of people surrounding one person who's speaking. The speaker is telling a story that everyone seems interested in. Naturally you want to get in on this, so you join the group.

"So then I went *back* to the store and found the woman." the speaker says. "And I told her she gave me the wrong shoes."

Of course you're confused. "What store?" you ask. "What woman? What's this about shoes?" And everyone turns and glares at you. Why? Because they've been listening to this story for a minute or two already. They already know about the store and the shoes. The speaker doesn't want to re-explain things that everyone else has already heard. They all want the speaker to continue the story.

There are unwritten social rules about entering a group situation. When a group is engaged in conversation, it's important to stand by quietly to get a sense of the conversation before you speak. Maybe you can guess what they're talking about, just by listening. Or maybe you can ask the speaker later to tell you the story again. Or maybe you won't understand what's going on. If you never hear the full story of the store and the shoes, it's no great loss. But if you just barge into a group and ask them to talk about what *you* want to talk about, that makes people think you're self-centered. They'll start to avoid you, and that's much worse than never getting the details on the shoe story.

Impulsive Thoughts

Do you ever interrupt yourself? You'll be talking about one subject and suddenly a new thought—on a totally different matter—will cross your mind. One client told me, "I interrupt myself so much that I even have daydreams during my daydreams!" When a new thought arrives, you feel you have to say it right away, and so you change subjects sometimes even mid-sentence. This isn't rude or selfish, like the habit of interrupting others, but it sure makes it difficult for others to follow.

In any conversation, as you speak, others try to think along with you. They track your statements and follow how the statements flow from one to another. But when a sentence seems to have no logical connection to the one before—they're lost. Although the thoughts and stories may seem unrelated to those listening, very often, there are connections for you. If you speak like that regularly, others may become overwhelmed, frustrated, or flooded by your impulsive thoughts. They may try to avoid conversations with you.

Impulsive Spending

Spending money impulsively often causes a great deal of trouble for those with AD/HD. Your spouse, your roommate, your children or parents—anyone whose finances are linked with yours—can become frustrated if you lack self-control, because your spending decisions directly affect them.

Clients I have worked with report an intense feeling that they can't live without some possession. They see something and they want it. And they want it NOW! Have you ever experienced impulses like that? Of course advertisers and merchants aren't going to help you any. They do everything they can to convince you that you need their products. They place their wares in special places as "impulse buys." They want you to find those objects irresistible. Even people without AD/HD get suckered into buying things they don't need. But it's a special problem for impulsive people.

By the time you get home with what you bought, you may even forget to bring it in from the car. Once you own it, you don't need it anymore. The impulse is momentary, strongest when you see the thing in front of you. In that moment, you don't think about your budget, you're thinking "gotta have it."

Helen was telling me of her problems with impulsive shopping. She was able to avoid going to the stores most of the time as a coping skill to minimize impulsive shopping. But Helen seemed to be helpless against the onslaught of home shopping options now available on the TV. She confessed to having an entire guest room filled with boxes from QVC and the Home Shopping Network, many of which were unopened.

As you might guess, these strong impulses put many people into financial binds. A paycheck gets spent in one night. Credit cards get maxed out. Cars get repossessed. Some families are forced into bankruptcy.

But beyond the money involved are the damaged relationships. Sometimes as a result of the impulsive purchases, you may be constantly putting yourself in a position where you need to borrow money. If so, you're probably taking advantage of your relationships with those who help you. When it happens again and again, people feel used. People have their limits. You can't expect them to bail you out when you're responding to your impulses. Once again, others will become angry and try to avoid you as they attribute your situation to your irresponsible, selfish behavior.

Even if you're not borrowing money, you also have a responsibility to consider the needs of others as well. Family members feel neglected and threatened when they have no say in your impulse expenditures.

I had a client with AD/HD who bought a house one day without telling his wife. They were just a middle-class couple, and they hadn't even been house-shopping. He was out driving and saw a sign for an open house. He went in, liked the house and thought that it would be a good idea to buy the house. He signed the papers and came home to tell his wife about it. Now that's an extreme case, but imagine his wife's feelings when she found out that this major purchase was made without her! She did not feel very important. In fact, she attributed his action to his lack of commitment to their relationship.

TIPS TO LIMIT IMPULSIVE SPENDING

1. Don't carry much cash with you if you don't have a specific reason.

2. Don't carry a charge card. It's too tempting for impulsive shoppers.

3. If you truly must have something, go back to your house to get the cash or your credit card. Then return to purchase the item if you still need it. You'll be surprised at the number of must-have, can't-live-without items that aren't worth a trip back to a store.

4. If you do buy items impulsively, wait a week before you unwrap or unpack them. Keep the receipt handy (taped on the box) so that you can return unwanted items. Again, you may be surprised with how quickly many of these items lose their value to you.

Impulsive Words

OTM—OTM that about sums up impulsive words. On The Mind—Out The Mouth[6]. Unfortunately, sometimes you say things that hurt people. You don't mean to, they just come out. In fact, sometimes you may even be trying to say something nice, but it doesn't come out that way. "That dress doesn't make you look so fat." You're trying to compliment the person, but the effect is the opposite. Maybe you've even lost friends over comments of yours that exploded in your face.

You may not realize that *everyone* has problems with this—AD/HD or not. Misunderstandings happen sometimes with awful results. But impulsive speakers are more prone to these problems because they don't filter their words well.

You see, everyone thinks negative things about other people (along with a lot of positive things), just as you do. We all know aunt Mabel is fat and cousin George smells bad and sister Mary sings off-key. But non-impulsive people filter out those thoughts before they get put into words—you may not. It's not that you're mean or hateful; you just have a hard time turning off the tap between your mind and your mouth.

When Jarryd was five (and not yet taking medication), I spent much time trying to teach him to think first before saying or doing something. His impulsivity had gotten him into a great deal of trouble. He had jumped out of our living room window in an attempt to fly—as he had just seen in the Superman show on television. He went wading in the reflecting pool at a local mall looking for pennies before I was able to catch him. He was a frequent visitor to our neighborhood hospital due to his many impulsive encounters. He often said things that hurt the feelings of others.

I explained to him that once you have a thought, you need to stop and decide whether or not it is a good idea before you say it or act on it. If it's a good idea—fine. If it's not, don't say it and don't do it. Jarryd looked puzzled, "There's no place to stop it, mom. It's just all one step. That part of my brain must be broken." At the age of five Jarryd had already begun educating me regarding the world of AD/HD.

If you have a coffeemaker, you know the importance of filters. The filter holds back the coffee grounds and only lets the liquid through. If you tried to make coffee without a filter, the grounds would go right through. You'd get a cup of coffee that had plenty of flavor—*too much* flavor—and it would be chewy. That is not what you're looking for in your morning blend.

The same thing happens when you don't filter your thoughts. They transform rapidly into words, making your comments . . . well, *chewier* than they need to be. Yes, you're just saying what you think. You're being honest, and some friends will find that refreshing. But not every thought needs to be spoken. In fact, many thoughts should not be spoken.

Mary had a problem with what she described as a "brutal honesty." She had fractured many social relationships, especially with family members, for "telling it like it is." One Christmas, Mary was given a lovely, expensive gift by her sister. Her sister had gone to a great deal of both effort and expense to try to surprise Mary with something that she hoped Mary would like. When Mary opened the gift she immediately blurted out, "Oh, I already have one."

Mary's sister was disappointed and felt unappreciated for all her efforts. "There's no sense buying you anything!" she huffed.

"Well," replied Mary, "if that's the way you feel about it, then don't!" And so the situation escalated out of control.

Although Mary's statement was true, it was not well worded or well timed. The situation would have had a very different ending if Mary had said, "I can't believe you went to all this trouble for me! That was so thoughtful of you. I know that you were trying to surprise me, and I really hate to

65

tell you this, but I already have one. I'm wondering could we go shopping together to exchange it. It would be fun to be with you. Again, I can't tell you how much I really appreciate your thoughtfulness!"

OR . . . She might have waited to discuss the fact that she already had one—at least until there was less of a crowd. In this situation, she could just say, "Why thank you! You are so thoughtful!"

OR . . . She could have quietly returned the present, without the receipt, along with all of the other "reverse shoppers" the day after Christmas. It probably wouldn't be difficult to find a store that carried the duplicate of the unwanted gift. In this case, she could still accept the gift graciously: "Why thank you! You are so thoughtful!" Her sister would never have to know she was returning it.

Recognize the power of your words.
Questions to consider _before_ speaking:
- What is the purpose of your statement?
- What do you think the other person will *think* about what you said?
- How do you think the other person will *feel* after you say this?
- Is this the best way to phrase it?

Physically Impulsive Behavior: Signs of Affection

Sometimes you just want to hug someone. Or touch a hand, or slap a back, or even give a kiss. Watch out for any of these impulses. They can be easily misunderstood, hurting your friendships and possibly even landing you in legal trouble.

People have physical boundaries. Our bodies are our most private possessions, and most people are careful about whom they touch, where, when, and how. This can be confusing because people have different boundaries. Some are very free with hugs while others resist them. Some are always touching your hand while others limit themselves to a handshake. How can you tell what's appropriate? Here are some tips to help you read the signals.

Is the other person initiating the physical overture? Are they starting all the hugging, arm touching, or backslapping? If so, you're probably safe. That means the other person finds it appropriate.

Is the other person returning your physical overture? Or are you doing all the touching? If they aren't returning the touch, that's a signal to avoid physical contact.

Is the other person resisting? If he or she pulls away from you or tenses as you approach, stop immediately—even if it seems awkward to do so. The person obviously doesn't want to be hugged, touched, or slapped.

Are you getting signals? Body language says a lot. How much space do people need around them? How close to you are they sitting or standing? When you move, do they move toward you or away? Do they open their bodies to you or turn away? These are all signals to help you understand what they want.

How do they behave with others? Do they hug or touch the other people? Observe them and see how physical they are in social situations. That will give you some clues about their comfort level. However, they may feel differently about you. So you still must be careful in your own physical expressions.

What's proper in the situation? In most workplaces, hugs and kisses are not welcome, even if co-workers are close friends. Anytime one person has more power or status, anything besides a handshake is probably inappropriate. In any situation, be aware of the possible implications of hugs, touches, and casual kisses between men and women —there are usually sexual overtones, which may be threatening to one or the other. As a general rule, *when in doubt, don't*. Unless you know for sure that the other person will welcome a hug, touch, kiss, or playful pat—restrain yourself.

Impulsive Verbal Anger

Sometimes you want to hurt people with your words. It's not a misunderstanding; you're really upset. Someone has hurt you in some way and you want to make them feel bad. So you may lash out with the angry words that are streaming through your mind. Not only do you lack a filter, you have a torrent of emotion flowing out of you. You're not thinking of consequences. You don't care at that moment how the other person will feel. You just need to vent.

But often the verbal explosion is just that—a big boom, followed by calm. Your angry thoughts are like a flash flood, rushing through gullies and then quickly drying up again. You got rid of your hurtful feelings, and now they're gone. You've said it all, and now it's over for you. It doesn't always happen like that, but many people with AD/HD can quickly get over their anger and move on.

However, the recipient of your explosion may not be so quick to get over it. You have launched verbal grenades at them, and now *they're* hurting. They may now be angry, and your quick dismissal of the problem may just fuel their anger. They may be confused about how you really feel—especially if you're smiling now after screaming a minute ago. They may be frustrated because you won't stay with the issue long enough for them to work through *their* feelings.

68

Karen, a woman with AD/HD, works in an office with several friends. One morning she marches up to Janice's desk and says, "I can't believe you didn't invite me to come to lunch with you yesterday. You are really a jerk." Slamming down a stack of photocopies, she goes on: "I don't know why you don't like me. It's not fair, you always include everybody else and leave me out." With that, she stomps away.

Janice calls after her, but then the phone rings and she has to attend to business the rest of the morning. But the whole time she's still upset about what Karen said. She didn't deserve those words. A jerk? The whole thing was just a little misunderstanding. Janice went out with some old friends in a different department, people Karen didn't know. Janice wasn't trying to exclude Karen, but maybe she should have explained it better.

So after Karen's outburst, Janice feels very confused, a bit guilty, and mostly angry. And she finds it hard to get her work done. As lunch time approaches, Janice wonders whether to try to patch things up with Karen. She decides not to. After the nasty things Karen said, Janice figures it's best to let both of them cool off for a day or two.

But suddenly Karen bounces up to Janice's desk. "Hi! I'm getting ready to go and eat," she says. "Do you want to come?"

Janice looks at her friend as if she just arrived from outer space. Less than an hour ago Karen was calling her a "jerk," and now she wants to do lunch. Is this the same person? Janice is even more confused, and then she gets angry. "If Karen thinks she can insult me like that and then pretend nothing happened, she's got another thing coming!"

Of course Karen doesn't realize there's a problem. She got rid of her anger earlier, and now she feels fine. She wants to have lunch again with her friend. But she doesn't realize

69

the lasting impact of her words. She dumped her feelings onto Janice, and now Janice has to dig her way out.

"Do you want to come?" Karen repeats.

"I don't think so," Janice responds coldly.

"Okay," Karen chirps. "Maybe tomorrow."

Your words have power. Especially angry words. Like a stone tossed into a stream, your words will have a ripple effect that lasts long after you have moved on. If you're hot-headed and prone to violent outbursts, it's important to understand that there's a person with feelings on the other end of your anger. Often they won't share their feelings with you, but that doesn't mean that feelings aren't there. They are often hurting from the impact of your words.

It doesn't matter whether or not you ever intended to hurt anyone. The excuse "That's just the way I am" is not acceptable. It does not erase their feelings. It's just not socially appropriate to firebomb others.

TIPS TO HELP CONTAIN ANGRY WORDS

1. Set a time and place to talk later, after you've had a chance to cool down.
2. Do something physical to help decrease your intensity.
3. Take a "time out" to prevent you from saying things you may regret.
   - Talk to yourself about what you want to say.

   - Write down the points you want to discuss.
   - Most importantly, write down your wish—the outcome you hope for.

Physically Impulsive Behavior: Aggressive

Sometimes your anger will feel so intense that you want to hit someone. Watch out for any of these impulses. Whenever you feel the impulse to hurt someone physically, hold back. As with your other impulses, you are not thinking about the consequences of your action. You have to let that moment pass.

TIPS TO MANAGE ANGER

1. Leave the area.

2. Get far away from the offending person.

3. Find a substitute action—hit a pillow or punching bag, run around the block.

4. Don't feed the impulse by focusing on your anger. Distract yourself. Turn on some soothing music or imagine yourself on a tropical island.

5. Seek counseling to learn ways to manage your anger.

6. Aggressive actions damage relationships and possibly even land you in legal trouble. Get help quick.

JUST THE FACTS

- Impulsivity is characterized by "Ready-Fire-Aim." Difficulty thinking first before saying or doing something.

- Impulsive behavior is often attributed to rudeness, arrogance, or self-centeredness.

- Impulsivity can add excitement to relationships.

- Impulsivity can overwhelm or frustrate others—especially the linear thinkers in your life.

- Some difficulties can include:
  Interrupting someone who is speaking;
  Impulsively entering a group;
  Impulsive thoughts;
  Impulsive spending;
  Impulsive words;
  Impulsive verbal anger;
  Physically impulsive behavior: affectionate;
  Physically impulsive behavior: aggressive.

NOTES
1. Kelly, K., & Luquet, M. (1998). ADD disorder in couples. In W. Luquet & M. Hannah, (Eds.). *Healing in the Relational Paradigm*, Washington, D.C.: Taylor & Francis. p.4
2. Whiteman, T., & Novotni, M. (1995). *Adult ADD: A reader-friendly guide to identifying, understanding, and treating adult attention deficit disorder*, Colorado Springs, Colorado: Pinion Press, p. 99.

3. Goldstein, S., and Goldstein, M. (1998). *Managing attention deficit hyperactivity disorder in children: A guide for practitioners*. New York: John Wiley & Sons. p.45.
4. Ibid, p.45
5. Mills, J. (1993). *Urgent reply*.. Marquette, Michigan: BOOM-ZING.
6. Lavoie, R. (1994) *Learning disabilities and social skills: last one picked...first one picked on*. Washington, D.C.: WETA-TV.

Chapter 5

Slow Down? Who, Me?: Hyperactivity

THE DICTIONARY DEFINES the prefix *hyper* as "over, above, more than the normal, excessive." Therefore, a *hyper*active person is one who takes the normal activity of life and makes it "over, above, more than the normal, excessive." In fact, that's a great description of many adults with AD/HD.

Not all people with AD/HD have symptoms of hyperactivity. There are different types of AD/HD. You might be AD/HD, predominately inattentive type, which means you have difficulty with inattention, and perhaps impulsivity but you're not hyperactive. Or you could have AD/HD predominantly hyperactive-impulsive type, which means you have difficulty with hperactivity and impulsivity, but not inattention. Finally, you may have AD/HD, combined type which means you have problems with inattention, hyperactivity, and impulsivity.

If your AD/HD does not include hyperactivity, you can skip this chapter. It won't apply to you. But for those of you who do show signs of hyperactivity—read on.

Excessive activity is the most visible sign of AD/HD and perhaps the most annoying to others. It's most noticeable in children with AD/HD, who run their parents and teachers ragged with their non-stop energy. "JUST SIT STILL!" You've probably heard that a few times in your life.

Some parents, after their child wanders off for the zillionth time, resort to a leash or a string tied around the child's wrist or waist. Onlookers show their disapproval—how could that child be treated like an animal?—but they don't know. They have no clue what it's like to have a child who will not—who *cannot*—stay in one place. Kids with AD/HD and hyperactivity can be little Houdinis—escape artists who defy containment. I know. I've got one.

My son Jarryd was a human tornado. Although we knew very early on that he had AD/HD, it was still difficult to keep up with him. He once came home from school confused because he knew some kids with AD/HD who weren't hyperactive. They were able to sit quietly while he wasn't. So I tried to explain to him about the different types of AD/HD—with and without hyperactivity.

Jarryd's face lit up. "I know what I have now," he said, smiling broadly. "I have ADRRRHD!"

Now I was confused. "Okay," I asked, "so what is ADRRRHD?"

"Attention Deficit Really, Really, Really Hyperactive Disorder!" he announced proudly.

Jarryd was right. In some cases hyperactivity deserves more than one letter in the acronym. It turns children into Energizer bunnies, and it drives moms and dads berserk. I've heard parents wish for a velcro wall they could just stick their kids on so they could relax for a few minutes. I can relate.

And I'm guessing that you can relate, from the other side of this struggle. You may have been the child who couldn't sit still, the one who wanted to be good but always

76

had a motor running. You may have been the student whose antics were frequently punished. Because you couldn't stay in one place, you were kept inside while the other kids went out for recess. (Does that make any sense?) You may have been labeled a problem child and lumped with the delinquents, even though you really wanted to obey. Your heart was always in the right place, even if your body wasn't.

Adult Hyperactivity

Some hyperactivity is outgrown as you age. You simply don't have the energy to keep up that pace. In adulthood the hyperactivity is generally more subtle. Not running around, but fidgeting. You might be tapping, scratching, shifting. You're restless. You have difficulty staying in a chair for long. As an adult, you don't have anyone chasing after you, but you can still irritate those around you. Your frequent movements can frustrate and distract your family, friends, and coworkers.

To be more specific, some symptoms of hyperactivity as described in the *DSM-IV,* which psychologists and psychiatrists use to diagnose, include:

- often leaves seat in situations where staying seated is expected;
- often fidgets with hands or feet or squirms in seat;
- subjective feeling of restlessness;
- often has difficulty engaging in leisure activities quietly; and
- often talks excessively

You may not have difficulty in all of the above areas. Some do, but others report just two or three of these problems. Still, any of these can result in social blunders, misunderstanding, or isolation.

In our society, the ability to remain seated or physically still is an important social skill. If you walk away in the middle of a conversation, get up and leave a meeting, or fidget, most people will think you're being rude.

People are programmed to try to make sense of the world—remember attribution theory. That is, they assume that others choose their actions, that they do what they do on purpose, for some explainable reason. So when you walk out of a meeting, they assume you're protesting what someone said. If you're squirming in your chair, they'll think you're bored or rude. They have to have some way to explain it, and if they're not aware of your AD/HD (and the hyperactivity that often goes along with it), how else can they understand your actions?

Likewise, if you're verbally hyperactive, people may think you're self-centered, and/or not interested in them. After all, you're just talking and talking without listening. If you cared about anyone else, they figure, you'd stop and listen to them. They probably don't realize your "motor mouth" is a symptom of AD/HD. You don't want to ignore others; you just can't seem to stop talking.

Hyperactivity, whether physical or verbal, can hurt your popularity. The more visible and more severe your symptoms, the harsher the social consequences.

In the social world, physically leaving a conversation or a meeting is perceived as a much bigger offense than merely fidgeting during a meeting or conversation. Likewise, if you internally feel restless, those feelings may go undetected by others. People can't see the hyperactivity in your brain, but if it leaks out in too many words, or too much movement—the social police will not be far behind in passing out fines for the violators.

So if your goal is to function better in society, you will want to try to move from the more obvious displays of hyperactivity to the less obvious. Those impulses will be there, but you may be able to choose less problematic ways of acting on them. If you can replace walking around with fidgeting, that's helpful. If you can stop fidgeting and merely feel internally restless, that will further improve your social interactions.

You can also work *with* each of those symptoms to make them less intrusive. For example, if you "almost always" leave conversations or meetings, those who meet with you regularly will learn that you can't function in meetings. They'll stop inviting you. Those who talk with you will start avoiding you, if you "almost always" leave conversations. The more you engage in inappropriate social behavior, the more people will attach you with your inappropriate behavior together. "Oh, there's the one-minute wonder," they'll say (or think) when you show up. In behavioral terms, that's "classical conditioning," when two things are paired together and the feelings of the one situation—your presence—are associated with the second—your leaving in mid-conversation.

John leaves an important meeting for a few minutes to stretch and move around and then comes back. He's not trying to bother anyone. All he knows is that he needs to move. He really can't think straight unless he takes a walk down the hall. So he does.

But his movement disrupts the flow of the meeting. His colleague Mary is in mid-sentence when John pushes his chair back and walks out, Mary takes it as a personal insult. The others are also annoyed at John's interruption.

79

And the same thing happens the following Wednesday at their weekly meeting, and the next Wednesday, and the next. Each time, John disrupts the meeting and annoys his colleagues. After three or four times, John finds it hard to talk with his colleagues on Thursday, Friday, Monday, or Tuesday. He passes them in the hall with a warm greeting, and they just sneer and mumble

What's going on? John's colleagues have been conditioned by John's annoying behavior in the meetings. Just seeing John now calls up their feelings of annoyance, so they're annoyed with him all the time.

You don't want to get caught up in that kind of conditioning. It's a basic logical equation.

> In a meeting, John = Disruption.
> Disruption of a meeting = Annoyance.
> Therefore, John = Annoyance.

What can John do? Well, he could attack the equation from the bottom or the top. He could work at trying to repair his relationships with the people he has annoyed. That would break the John = Annoyance link. He could say, "I'm not just a disrupter, I'm a nice guy. Here, see what a fun person I am." This can be difficult if people are already annoyed, but many people with AD/HD are able to do this. They use their winning, energetic personalities to make friends even when their behavior is bothersome.

He could also explain to people about AD/HD and how his hyperactivity makes it difficult to remain seated. If he's dealing with kind people, this may restore some relationships. Good people will cut you some slack. Once they have a reason for the disruptive behavior, they won't be as likely to attribute it to all sorts of negative motives. But it's still disruptive to leave a meeting, so John will need to work with his colleagues to find ways to annoy them less.

The most effective way to break the conditioning and to become less annoying, is to stop leaving meetings, or even to do so less often. If John could discipline himself to stay in one meeting a month, then two, then three—he'd make a huge improvement. Maybe he stays in the meeting and fidgets, which is less disruptive than leaving. Perhaps he could always sit by the door so that he could make a less disruptive exit. Or maybe he talks the others into taking a break halfway through the meeting so everyone can stretch their legs.

The bottom line is simple, though it's a challenge. It's better to have less disruptive behavior, than a more disruptive behavior. And it is better to have a low-frequency disruptive behavior, rather than a high-frequency disruptive behavior.

Let's now look at the different ways hyperactivity can appear in adults with AD/HD.

Often leaves seat in situations where staying seated is expected

Children with AD/HD are notorious for not staying seated. In classroom situations, the ability to remain seated is critical. Children are seated at desks and required to pay attention to the teacher. Punishment is exacted upon those who keep getting up. For harried teachers and distracted students, it sometimes seems that school is all about sitting down and being quiet—two activities that are especially difficult for hyperactive kids with AD/HD.

Some of you have the same difficulty. Physical hyperactivity of some type often persists through adulthood. The most hyperactive adults gravitate toward jobs that involve motion—delivery, sales, construction. But everyone faces situations where they have to sit down for a while—church, plane rides, banquets, heart-to-heart conversations—and hyperactive adults may have a difficult time.

81

"I must have quit more than 120 jobs in the past 20 years," said Dave, an adult with AD/HD, to his support group. "Most of the time I had to quit because I couldn't stand it any longer. It's difficult being an engineer because everyone seems to want me to stay seated in my little cubby hole all day long."

Dave was frequently reprimanded for his poor work habits, probably because he often left his work station and wandered around. It looked like he was goofing off, but he needed those walks to refuel. Afterward he could throw himself into his work with renewed energy.

But his bosses kept insisting that he stay at his desk. They felt that his up-and-down, "Jack in the Box" behavior was disruptive to the other employees and limited the amount of time Dave was actually working. Though the quality of his work was excellent, Dave was not viewed as a productive employee.

"I don't know how anyone can be expected to work under such inhumane conditions!" he complained.

AD/HD symptoms are often misunderstood and misinterpreted. Dave was struggling with job difficulties, poor self-esteem, as well as depression, primarily because he found it difficult to remain seated for long periods of time. The price for breaking the social rules can be steep!

Some hyperactive adults learn to avoid situations in which they can't move about freely.

Megan would not attend theater, ballet, or concert events with her friends because she wouldn't be able to get up and move around during the performances. At times she would try to get an aisle seat in the back, so she could slip out unnoticed and walk around more easily. Sometimes that worked.

Other times, the social police were watching—the ushers or her friends would make faces or ask her to please remain in her seat so the performers and other patrons would not be disturbed.

Most of the time, it was not worth the risk of embarrassment to attend any long sit-down events. She avoided many social opportunities with her friends. Her friends got the idea that she didn't like them. They attributed her nonattendance as a lack of desire to be with them, rather than a struggle with hyperactivity.

Often fidgets with hands or feet or squirms in seat

Fidgeting varies from person to person, but it generally involves movements of legs, arms, fingers, or butt. Some people tap their fingers, others tap their feet, still others tap objects. Some may shift their weight in a chair or cross and uncross their legs. All these movements are more subtle than leaving your seat and walking around, but they can still distract people.

Socially, it's important to look as if you are listening. And fidgeting makes it look as if you're not. When you look attentive, you allow other people to talk comfortably—they don't feel that they have to fight to hold your interest. But how will people feel if you're tapping your foot or playing finger games and not even looking at them as they talk? Unappreciated, to say the least. They feel that you don't care about what they're saying. Maybe you *are* listening. Maybe you can repeat everything the person just said. It doesn't matter. Your actions send a message. Your actions imply, "I'm more interested in checking my watch or flipping through the newspaper than in what you're saying."

83

Not only does fidgeting make it look like you're not paying attention, it can also make it very difficult for others to pay attention to *you*. All those movements can distract people from what you're saying.

Our old friend, John, is asked to give a report at the weekly meeting. This is great for him because he gets to stand up and walk around while giving this presentation. No need to leave in the middle.

But his hyperactivity is still in force, and he paces and shifted his weight as he talks. The group feels as if they're watching a tennis match— on a ship. John also tinkers with his watch. These are absentminded mannerisms—turning the watchband around, pulling at it, grasping his wrist—but they're quite distracting to others.

Later he asks a co-worker what she thought of the ideas he presented at the meeting.

"I didn't really follow it very well," she apologizes. "I'm sorry. . . . but where did you get that watch?"

Excessive fidgeting can negatively impact good communication, whether in a group or one-to-one, whether you're speaking or listening. While it's not quite as rude as walking away, fidgeting still sends a message of disinterest, which can be offensive. It always draws attention away from the words being said—your words or the other person's.

Often talks excessively

What happens when you're the one talking? How does hyperactivity become a problem?

Often those with AD/HD flood the other person with words, overwhelming them and not allowing others a chance to respond. Listeners can feel as if they've been run over by

84

a train. Obviously, this does not produce a comfortable conversational environment. No one can be an active conversational partner when they can't participate. And not only do some people with AD/HD speak a lot, they often speak too quickly and too loudly—all social blunders.

At an AD/HD conference in California, Linda told me about her difficulty with interpersonal relationships. Her main struggle with AD/HD was in this matter of excessive talking. "I don't want to talk too much," she said. "Often I don't even know that I'm talking too much, but everyone always tells me I talk too much, so I guess that I do talk too much. I don't know how to stop talking too much—you know, there is no place to go if you talk too much. If someone eats too much they can go to Weight Watchers, if someone gambles too much there is Gamblers Anonymous, if someone drinks too much they can go to Alcoholics Anonymous, but where do you go if you talk too much?"

It was easy to see Linda's pain due to her verbal hyperactivity. It was also easy to see that she was paying the price of social isolation for her failure to obey the social rules.

Adults with AD/HD keep telling me they have so much to say that they try to say it all at once, because they're afraid they'll forget what they wanted to say. But this behavior often frustrates the listener. On the receiving end of the conversation, the person can feel used, just a sounding board. Your rapid torrent of words makes them feel that you don't want their input, you just want to get the words out. More importantly, your rapid torrent of words makes them feel that you don't value them.

85

That's why people avoid excessive talkers. There's no "off" switch. There's no way to gracefully exit. Normally a person would wait for a pause and say, "Hey, I've got to run." But the excessive talker leaves no pauses. Often the listener has to be rude—interrupting or just walking away—in order to escape.

Subjective feeling of restlessness

Often adults with AD/HD can contain their physical and verbal manifestations of hyperactivity. But even though others don't see or hear the hyperactivity, it's still going on . . . inside. Even while containing it, the person often feels an internal sense of movement and restlessness.

It's an ongoing battle: the inner urge to move *vs.* the social norms for stillness. Trying to manage this restlessness, you may move from task to task as you get bored with one after another. You feel a strong urge to explore, to find new adventures. Thrill seeking is common among those with AD/HD.

At times this restlessness can be viewed as a positive behavior. Moving from task to task or idea to idea can be stimulating and fun at times. Our culture hails the adventurer as a person of courage. But the same sense of restlessness can often leave you feeling unfulfilled and dissatisfied as you fail time and time again to find contentment. Those closest to you can also become frustrated with the restlessness, and worn out by the pursuit of new thrills.

Bob and Sarah had come in for counseling. They knew that something was wrong with their relationship. Although they had been married for 10 years, they were almost at the point of considering divorce. Sarah said she was tired of all the changes. "Bob never finishes anything!" she complained. "He starts something and then he changes his mind. Or he tries to find another way to do it. Our house is overflowing with unfinished projects!"

Bob felt that Sarah had become boring. They had completely different ideas of fun. She did not consider it fun to jump from planes or race cars. He did. Bob's mind was always open to new possibilities. He loved to think of new and better ways to do things, but Sarah didn't seem to appreciate his creativity. All Sarah did was complain about unfinished projects.

In counseling, Bob and Sarah worked together to understand the impact of AD/HD on their relationship. Once they understood what was happening to them and why, they were able to negotiate compromises that made them both happy.

Often has difficulty in engaging in leisure activities quietly

Intimacy is one of the most important of the social skills. But intimacy is usually created and developed during the quiet times—and quiet times can be the worst moments for those of you struggling with hyperactivity.

The words "Let's go on vacation . . . just rest and relax and watch the waves all day" can create a panic. Everyone else in the family may be relaxing, but that's when the hyperactive mind goes into overdrive. Without external stimulation, the brain creates its own—and there's no shortage. Random thoughts and new ideas rush to fill any quiet corner. It's difficult to concentrate on relaxing when your body wants to move.

"Let's just be alone together, turn off everything else, and focus on each other." It sounds beautifully intimate, but it scares many with AD/HD. It's difficult to "turn off everything else." Whenever an outside distraction gets turned off, it seems like two internal ones click on. And so, in a way, it's impossible to be alone with anyone, because you always have a handful of other thoughts hanging out with you. To be forced to "focus on each other" when focus is your whole problem—well, that's difficult.

Alone with the one you love, you have no excuses not to relax and enjoy your leisure time. However, it may actually be hard work for you to relax

If you have AD/HD with hyperactivity, this quiet, leisure activity stuff is not all it's cracked up to be! And so the people closest to you need to understand how difficult it is for you to do any typical "relaxing." For you, it's a lot of work! So if you do choose to participate in a relaxing leisure activity, they should appreciate the effort you're making to grow the relationship. Perhaps next time they'll let *you* choose a relaxing leisure activity. Bungee jumping, anyone?

JUST THE FACTS

- Hyperactivity is described as over, above, excessive, more than the normal activity level.

- Excessive activity is the most visible sign of AD/HD, and most annoying to others.

- The five symptoms of hyperactivity are:
  - Often leaves seat in situations where staying seated is expected
  - Often fidgets with hands or feet or squirms in seat
  - Subjective feeling of restlessness
  - Often has difficulty engaging in leisure activities quietly
  - Often talks excessively

- All of these behaviors can send negative messages to others, creating difficulty in social relationships.

- It's better to have a less disruptive behavior, than a more disruptive behavior. And it is better to have a low-frequency disruptive behavior, rather than a high-frequency disruptive behavior.

Chapter 6

Did You Say
We'd Meet on Saturday?
I Thought You Said Tuesday!:
Disorganization

LIFE IS FULL of things to do, papers to file, and dates to remember. Deadlines, appointments, and anniversaries can crowd anyone's mind. The pace of life seems to be so fast these days, how can anyone stay organized? But as hectic as life gets for the general public—it's worse for most people with AD/HD.

Most, not all. Some of you are very organized, sometimes even too organized. Some learn habits or develop patterns that keep your lives well-structured. If you're like that, and you have no problem with organization, you can just skip this chapter.

However, disorganization is a major symptom of AD/HD. If your life is in disorder, that's not unusual.

My son, Jarryd, still struggles in the area of organization. At times he has worked for several hours on a school project and then forgotten to take it to school, or he has packed

91

his lunch but left it in the refrigerator. Usually we do not rescue him. In trying to help him become responsible and learn to manage his AD/HD, we generally let him deal with the natural consequences of his actions. There was, however, one exception . . .

Jarryd generally rushes out the door in the morning, catching a ride with my husband to school. Although he is supposed to be packed up the night before, there's often some last-minute rushing. One day I got a call at 7:10 a.m., shortly after they had left. It was Jarryd.

"Mom," he said, "I don't want you to give me any of that responsibility lecture crap this time. I need you to bring something to school for me now, and you can't tell me to take responsibility for my actions this time."

The urgency in his voice let me know this was very important to him. "You seem upset, Jarryd, what did you forget?"

"My shoes!"

Puzzled, I repeated, "Your shoes? Did you need to bring extra shoes to school for gym class or something?"

"No. I'm standing in the principal's office in my stocking feet, and I need you to bring my shoes. You will, won't you?"

I assured him that I would bring his shoes immediately. I couldn't help asking, "How could you forget your shoes?"

He told me that he frequently finishes dressing in the car on the way to school, which often means running out to the car in his socks. This time, he had forgotten to grab his shoes on the way out so he was dropped off at school shoeless.

What important items have you forgotten? Most people with AD/HD have a number of stories of things they've left behind.

When you forget things, others often think you're being irresponsible. Disorganization can cause hurt feelings and angry outbursts. It can damage trust.

The strange thing is, AD/HD is unpredictable. This makes it even harder for others to understand. You can and do remember a great number of things. You can be very structured for six hours and then lose it in the seventh. You can remember the words to the Gettysburg Address and forget your own address. This on-again, off-again quality works against you. When you're "off," people may think you're intentionally forgetting things. "Since you can usually stay

93

organized," they think, "this mess-up must mean you don't care about this." Or your spouse might assume, "If you can remember all your deadlines at work, you must be able to remember our anniversary." Since people know you *can* be organized at times, they attribute your lapses to a lack of motivation or a defect of character.

You're irresponsible.

I can't trust you.

You're lazy.

You don't care about me, or else you wouldn't have forgotten our date.

Attribution theory strikes again! People attribute the worst to you because they don't understand the unpredictable nature of AD/HD.

Overcompensation

You may structure your life quite rigidly. You've learned certain patterns that allow you to keep your life organized. Ironically, you can seem *too* rigid to others. Friends may tell you to loosen up, relax, do something different for a change. But you fear that if you deviate from your routine, everything will fall apart. Your rigidity is what holds you together.

Samantha would pay the bills for her company every Friday. For as long as she worked at the company, Friday was when she paid the bills. Once, when her new boss approached her on a Tuesday to pay a bill, Samantha flew into a fit of rage. Her boss could not understand her rigid behavior and considered putting her on disciplinary notice. Samantha, who struggled with AD/HD, had found comfort in routines. Through the external structure of her unwavering schedule, she was able to keep her world in order. The boss was asking her to change that structure, and she feared that

94

the change would unleash a whole set of uncertainties. Her response came out of that fear. Unfortunately, her boss didn't understand that Samantha was managing her AD/HD by following a pattern. He thought that paying a bill on Tuesday was no big deal. Because he didn't understand, the boss considered her a bit obsessive, rigid and strange, when she was just trying to cope.

Routines, policies, and procedures offer comfort for some to manage the disorganization of AD/HD. Instead of remembering 10 individual actions, you learn one routine. Many learn to make lists and follow them in order—one thing at a time. If you look at the whole list, you'll be overwhelmed by all the items that demand your attention. But one by one, you can conquer them.

Frank worked as an inspector for an airline. I asked him how he could handle such a highly focused, disciplined, detail-oriented job when he had AD/HD. "It's pretty easy for me," he answered, "since I really have no choices. I just have to follow a list, and I go through the list in order."

The structure of the job gave Frank comfort and success. If he had less external structure—for instance, if he had to decide which details to check first—he'd probably have a hard time. The flood of possibilities might overwhelm him. But the step-by-step routine arranges his workload for him. He doesn't have to organize himself.

I have found that many folks are quite resourceful in finding the routines they need to organize their lives. Through trial-and-error, hit-and-miss, they learn patterns that give them at least a minimum structure. Some, like Samantha, set up strict policies for their daily work. Some, like Frank, move toward jobs that impose that kind of organization on them. But organization doesn't come easily to them. Without those routines, they'd be lost. And often there are things that slip through the cracks of their routines. The boss wants a bill paid on the "wrong" day, or perhaps Frank's airline changes their system. If the pattern changes, you may have difficulty.

We don't know how Samantha and Frank organize their lives at home. Many people, after a high-structure day at work, like to kick back and relax at home. For disorganized people, that may mean chaotic relationships, messy homes, and uncertain schedules.

Degrees of Difficulty

What's wrong with having a messy home? Perhaps nothing. Disorganization can be lived with, but it can also cause problems in your relationships, your work, and the activities of your everyday life. You don't have to become a neat freak or clock-puncher, if that's not in your nature. But you'll probably want to ease the problems that go along with disorganization.

And of course folks with AD/HD aren't the only disorganized people in the world. Everyone can have some difficulties in this area. Think of disorganization on a scale from one to ten:

Disorganization								Organization	
1	2	3	4	5	6	7	8	9	10
Undependable							Super Organized		
Forgets way too much							Never forgets		

Around the low end of the scale, maybe 3 or 4, are people who miss appointments occasionally, are late once in a while due to poor planning, or miss making a payment here and there. Many people with AD/HD are on the high end of the scale, 7 or higher. You may miss about 30 percent of your appointments, run late almost half the time, and quite often forget to pay your bills. On the low end of the scale, disorganization is an occasional annoyance, but it does not have a significantly negative impact on relationships. On the high end of the scale, relationships frequently seem to be negatively affected by difficulties with disorganization.

I needed to call someone, but I had lost the number. Jim Reisinger, the head of ADDien, had given me this number and I had jotted it down, but now I couldn't find the paper. I generally don't misplace papers, but this one had vanished. After searching high and low, I sheepishly called Jim back and asked for the number again.

Jim, who has AD/HD himself, was thrilled that I had misplaced the number. "It's nice for you to have an ADD moment," he teased. "Now imagine that this happens to you every day. Now imagine that this happens to you several times every day. That's what living with AD/HD can be like."

I appreciated his insight. These "ADD moments" happen to everyone, but they're a regular problem for many people with AD/HD.

Let's take a look at several different areas of organizational difficulty.

Time

"Time, in general, seems to be somewhat elusive for those with ADD. It is an abstract concept, separated from their daily lives. Time seems indefinite, infinite, and unable to be sliced into neat one-hour components."[1] Those with AD/HD are often in the wrong places at the wrong times. You may have problems with promptness, sending bills on time, and keeping appointments. This clearly affects others in your life. The person on the receiving end of a missed date often feels slighted. And that makes it difficult to build and maintain relationships.

Randolph found himself alone on Saturday night . . . again. The guys don't seem to call him anymore. Everyone seems to make excuses when he asks about their plans. Thinking back, Randolph realized that his friends seemed to be mad at him ever since they missed getting into the new "Star Wars" movie because they were waiting for him. At the time, it didn't seem like that big a deal to Randolph. His friends all knew that he was generally late. He thought they accepted this fact—that was just the way he was. But maybe they were actually mad at him for being late all the time.

Randolph intended to be on time, but he always found one more thing to try to do before he left. And that one more thing generally turned into another, and yet another. Somehow he always seemed to run out of time.

All the other guys cleared their plans to meet on time. Although they liked Randolph, they were tired of putting up with his irresponsible behavior. Why should they all have to wait because he wanted to do something else first? They too had other things to do, but they were responsible. They didn't keep others waiting. What was wrong with Randolph? He didn't seem to respect them or their schedules. He seemed to be so self-centered that he only cared about what he wanted to do. It didn't seem to bother him when he kept everyone waiting like hostages. He did it all the time.

After the "Star Wars" fiasco, something they had planned for weeks, they finally decided they'd had enough. They were tired of being inconvenienced as a result of Randolph's irresponsible behavior.

Time problems can create many misunderstandings. If you're chronically late, people will think you don't want to see them. That's attribution theory, pure and simple. "If this meeting were truly important to you, people think, you'd make it a point to be there on time." They attribute your tardiness or absence to a lack of caring rather than your AD/HD-related disorganization.

Unfortunately, understanding attribution theory doesn't solve every problem. "I still can get annoyed with my friend Suzy. I know she has AD/HD. I understand it. I know she doesn't want to miss meetings, but I've also learned I can't count on her to be there when she says she will. That's a limitation of our relationship."

If your social life and your relationships are suffering because of time management difficulties, consider making this a goal to work on. There are many strategies that can help you become more time conscious—even with AD/HD.

Money

Each of us has to be a bit of an accountant as we manage our finances. Whether we're investing in stocks, paying the rent, or grocery shopping, we need a certain amount of organization and discipline—qualities that frustrate many people with AD/HD. Perhaps you get into financial trouble due to disorganization and mismanagement.

In an AD/HD support group I lead, people were discussing the number of times their water, electric, and/or phone had been shut off. The stories flew fast and furious. "Right now I have no power at home," said one with an embarrassed shrug. "I guess I just misplaced the bill. It never got paid." Others nodded. They had done that, too.

They got more excited as they shared their difficulty keeping a checking account balanced. "I just call the bank and ask them how much money I have," said one woman. "I figure they should know."

"But what about outstanding checks?" I asked. I got a blank look. "You know, checks you've written that haven't cleared yet. Shouldn't you subtract those, too?"

Most in the group had difficulty with bounced checks. Many had let their spouses take over the family's money management. In fact, when it came time to pay for the session, most of the participants pulled out checks that had been pre-written by their partners (though a few had inadvertently left their checks at home).

Even in non-AD/HD homes, money can be a major source of marital discord. Imagine how difficult it is when one partner misplaces bills or paychecks, spends impulsively, or lines the canary cage with tax documents. Money issues can damage other relationships too. Did you pay your neighbor back for those concert tickets? Maybe you honestly forgot, but your neighbor may think you're intentionally shirking your debt. How you handle money impacts your relationships with others. If this is causing your difficulty—it's a great goal to work on.

Stuff

Piles, piles, and more piles.

Lynn Weiss, an AD/HD author and lecturer, had once said that you can tell someone with AD/HD by the three P's— Piles, Procrastination, and lost Potential.

It's not just information that's disorganized in the AD/HD mind, it's *also stuff.* Most people will look at something and put it in a certain category. "This is a hammer; it's a tool; it belongs in the toolbox." But you may see three other uses for that same object. "That hammer would be a great paperweight or doorstop, and it can help me open jars." The hammer "belongs" on the desk or by the door or in the kitchen. Because it's so hard to put it in just one category, it gets put aside to deal with later. The hammer never makes it to the toolbox. It sits out on the table, ready to be employed in any of its possible uses which add to the piles

This is called "out-of-the-box" thinking. And that's one reason why many people with AD/HD are often artists, inventors, and entrepreneurs. Conventional categories are defied and new options eagerly explored. But this process can be messy!

A printed piece of paper, with all its information, is teeming with possibilities. You don't want to limit those possibilities by filing it away in a particular folder, in a particular cabinet. Yes, it has to be dealt with—but not just yet. "I'll get to that later" is a common thought. As a result, the paper gets piled, and the pile grows.

The story is told of an employee who went to the company psychologist. "I think I might have AD/HD," he said. "They tell me you have a simple three-question test that will tell me for sure."

101

The psychologist replied, "Sure, just look at your desk.
Question 1: How many piles of stuff do you have there?
Question 2: How big are the piles?
Question 3: How old is the stuff at the bottom?"

You may be messy and cluttered. "Cleaning" may just involve stacking the piles more neatly. Of course this can cause tension at home. But it can also make you embarrassed to have company over. You may even turn down social engagements—not going out to other people's homes because you feel you can't reciprocate. Your own home is too disheveled. Clutter becomes a barrier to social relationships.

Lost in the piles are often important letters from old friends, invitations requiring RSVP, and new addresses of those who have moved. If you've been wondering, "Whatever happened to old so-and-so?", the answer may be buried under several layers of paper. Once again, disorganization contributes to social isolation.

Marie's husband wanted a divorce. Among other reasons, he was tired of dealing with her perpetual disorganization. Marie realized the relationship was over, but was hesitant to get a divorce.

If I get a divorce, she reasoned, that means we must sell the house. In order to sell the house, I have to clear out the piles. I just can't do that!

As she discussed her situation, she told of "thigh high piles" in many rooms with boxes stacked along the perimeter. She described rooms in which there was only a small path to walk in between towers of boxes. She didn't even know what the boxes contained.

102

Marie was overwhelmed with the idea of dealing with a lifetime of disorganization. In discussions with her, it became evident that she had been struggling with AD/HD. Her actions suddenly made sense. Unfortunately, she was not able to save the marriage, but she was able to clear out the piles in her house. In addition, she developed an organizational system at work.

Disorganization may cause you to lose important documents, clothing, or keys. I've even heard about lost cars. Misplacing things may infuriate others in your life. They may consider you irresponsible or untrustworthy. They may be reluctant to lend you things.

Learning to manage stuff can be difficult with AD/HD—but not impossible. There are a number of strategies that can help.

Disorganization of self

The value of a first impression is significant and long-lasting. Because some people with AD/HD are often rushed, they may not always have time to take showers and engage in other personal hygiene and grooming activities. This is *definitely* not true for all adults with AD/HD—just some. But if you're racing to catch a train, you might not have time to brush your teeth. Gathering your briefcase and keys, you might forget to comb your hair. As a result, some may have an unkempt physical appearance. Clothes may be mismatched or wrinkled.

This disheveled appearance is not always accidental. Some folks with AD/HD apply their "out-of-the box" thinking to their wardrobe. You may put together an outfit with plaids and stripes. Why not? You may dye your hair blue or wear lots of jewelry or make-up. Fitting in can get boring.

103

Nowadays creative fashion can be accepted, even applauded—in certain settings. On a college campus anything goes, but if you're trying to get ahead in the business world, mismatched clothing suggests that you're not a match for the company. People can judge you harshly based on your appearance. They often attribute all sorts of negative qualities to people who don't look right.

Difficulties in your appearance can limit opportunities for social relationships to develop. Others may not take the time to get to know you, if your appearance is strange.

Forgetting responsibilities

Relationships involve responsibilities. It may be your turn to pick up the kids or get milk on the way home from work. At times, you may forget these duties. This "irresponsible behavior" presents many challenges for relationships.

AD/HD may also cause an imbalance in social relationships, which can lead to hurt and angry feelings. In her book, *The Dance of Intimacy*, Harriet Lerner describes a cycle of overfunctioning (doing too much) and underfunctioning (not doing enough). People without AD/HD often overfunction, to compensate for the person with AD/HD. They pick up the slack, but often way more than they want to. If the person with AD/HD forgets to do something, the overfunctioner may quickly take over. In turn, people with AD/HD may underfunction—not doing all that they can because they know that the other person will.[2]

This unbalanced arrangement occurs in many relationships—both those with and without AD/HD. It involves a variety of social interactions—such as paying for meals, driving the kids, cleaning the house, and answering the phone. The overfunctioning person may at first willingly step in to fill the gaps caused by the other person's AD/HD. But often

104

these efforts go unnoticed. (Noticing is not something folks with AD/HD do well.) As a result, the overfunctioners may feel unappreciated and unvalued.

The continuing lack of balance in the relationship can create anger and resentment on the part of the overfunctioner, as you might expect. But, when these feelings are expressed, the underfunctioner can feel hurt and angry as well.

In trying to balance such relationships, people need to be realistic about the limitations of AD/HD. It may make sense to have the person without AD/HD balance the checkbook, but in balancing the relationship, there should be other jobs that the person with AD/HD can do.

Unfinished projects

Due to disorganization, you may not always finish what you are supposed to, when you are supposed to. Deadlines can be difficult.

TOP FIVE REASONS
I'm Not Finished because...
1. *I don't remember the project.*
2. *I've lost an important part for the project.*
3. *I've lost the project.*
4. *I've lost interest in the project.*
5. *A new project has caught my eye.*

The term *attention deficit* isn't exactly descriptive. You may have a hard time focusing on one thing, because your mind is entertaining so many ideas. Most times you're actually attending to a number of things at once. You might say it's a very active attention span. Given this CB scanner approach to viewing life, many tasks go unfinished.

Unfinished tasks can have negative implications in the workplace. Employers may be reluctant to give important projects to you.

As with other symptoms of AD/HD, unmanaged disorganization can create social difficulties. Rejection, social isolation, and perhaps even being passed over for a promotion are just some of the prices that can be paid for disorganization.

Disorganized folks with AD/HD may need some outside help. But there are definitely strategies that can be effective in helping you meet those deadlines and finish those tasks!

JUST THE FACTS

- Everyone can have difficulties with organization, but people with AD/HD seem to have more than their fair share.

- Some can have problems with being too organized and rigid.

- Organizational difficulties place stress on relationships. Others can become frustrated or angry because they attribute your disorganization to you being self-centered, untrustworthy and/or irresponsible.

- Disorganization can cause problems in the areas of:
  1. Time: Wrong place/ wrong time. Difficulties with promptness, sending bills on time, and keeping appointments.

106

2. *Money*: Difficulty balancing checkbooks, paying bills on time, and planning finances.

3. *Stuff* becomes more difficult to manage with AD/HD because of out-of-the-box thinking. Clutter can become a barrier to social relationships. Important items are sometimes lost.

4. *Appearance*: Other may judge you harshly if you appear disorganized, disheveled, or just different.

5. *Forgetting responsibilities to others*: People become upset if you don't do what you say you will do. Overfunctioning—others often do too much to take up the slack Underfunctioning—you may contribute too little to the relationship.

6. *Unfinished Projects*: Disorganization and shifting attention can result in moving from one unfinished project to another.

NOTES

1.   Whiteman, T. , & Novotni, M. (1995). *Adult ADD: A reader-friendly guide to identifying, understanding, and treating adult attention deficit disorder*, Colorado Springs: Pinion Press. p. 186-187.

2.   Lerner, H. (1989). *The dance of intimacy*. New York: Harper & Row.

Part Three

Discovering the Social Skills You Need

Chapter 7

Please, Thank You, and Would You Pass the Mashed Potatoes?: Manners/Etiquette

"I WAS RAISED in the South. It was a real big thing for all families to have a book of etiquette in the house. And my mom used to go over it all the time. Then I moved away. I never heard anyone speaking of this anymore."

A woman I met at a conference was telling me of her experiences with manners and AD/HD.

"We knew what to say, when to say it, and what to do when we went to someone's house. But there's nothing anymore, and we do bad things. We go to eat and we eat terribly. And you know, girl, we got our arms on the table," everything has just gotten sloppy. We don't have anything to reference. We don't have those old fashion values. It's out of balance. It seems like, in general, society has gotten lax about social rules and etiquette. And for whatever reason, people with ADD seem to be worse."

111

Manners are Basically Rules of Niceness

That's right—there are rules. There are right ways to do things and wrong ways to do things. It's not enough to *try* to be nice, if you're breaking the rules. Whatever your intentions are, if you don't mind your manners, people will still think you're not being nice.

These social rules can be obscure at times. But when you break one, there are awkward silences and stares. You know that you have done something wrong but often you may not know what you did. (And strangely, it's considered rude to *tell* others what they've done wrong. People are just expected to *know*.)

Someone shakes your hand and says, "Hi, I'm John." That means you're supposed to give your name in return. If someone says, "You look nice today," you need to acknowledge the compliment and thank the person for it.

Imagine that your neighbor sees you in the driveway and asks, "What's wrong? You walked right past me in the supermarket and didn't say hello. Are you mad at me or something?" Of course, you're not mad. You remember seeing your neighbor, but you had other things on your mind. You didn't even think about greeting her at the time.

Feuds have started from simple omissions like this. When you see someone you know, you say hello and when you leave say goodbye. If you don't, they may be offended. People expect you to greet them. Without those basic manners, they'll assume you're upset with them or rude.

A friend stops you and asks, "What happened? We were talking at the party last week, and then Barb joined us and you just left. She thought you didn't like her." You probably

112

just saw someone else you wanted to talk to, but to drift away without a word—that's a way to lose friends. What else is Barb supposed to think when she steps into the circle and you step out?

Since you have difficulties with inattention, hyperactivity, and/or impulsivity, you tend to have more difficulty than others picking up these social rules. The finer points of manners and etiquette may have passed you by, and so you break these "rules" without realizing it. Others may interpret your actions as thoughtless or selfish, even if you had good intentions.

You need to learn good manners so others can get to know you and find out what a nice person you really are.

But why can't people just accept you the way you are? Why do you have to put on this act? A writer named Mary Mitchell answered that question in a column she calls "Ms. Demeanor."

"Dear Ms. Demeanor:

My mother is always telling me to mind my manners because nobody will want to hang out with me if my manners are bad. I say that doesn't matter.

I want my friends to like me because I'm a good person, which I am.

If somebody likes me just because I know good manners, I don't need to be their friend.

—Scott, 14

Dear Scott:

. . . I understand exactly what you mean. People should judge us based on our values, our moral code, and our integrity. Ultimately they do.

113

It's just that you have to get to know someone to find out about all that. Sometimes we behave in ways that make others reluctant to take that step, so they never find out what sterling people we are. Everybody loses then.

Unfortunately, first impressions are as enduring as concrete. We judge others based on very superficial things. In a perfect world, these perceptions shouldn't matter. The world is far from perfect, though. . . . We do form opinions based on impressions. Often those impressions have nothing to do with truth and reality. That's why it makes sense to learn good manners and to practice them. When you learn how to deal with others, life usually is happier.

It's really your personal choice. Once you know the downside, the risks in terms of successful relationships become the price you're willing to pay. I happen not to believe it's worth it." [1]

Please understand, I'm not talking about using the proper salad fork and extending your pinkie as you sip your drink. I'm talking about using words and actions that show respect and let people know you value them. These are great habits to get into. When you act with manners, you're practicing the Golden Rule—treating others the way you'd like them to treat you. That kind of behavior will win you friends and deepen your relationships.

Let's look at some of these basic manners.

Please

Sometimes in the rush of the moment or amidst swirling thoughts, you may forget to use "extra words" like *please* and *thank you*. Extra words take time, and you may hurry. But this economy of words can cost you dearly. You may save a few words, but lose lots of points in the relationship.

114

"Would you **please** get me a glass of water?" Sounds a million times better than, "Get me some water." The first sounds like a polite request. The second sounds more like a command. The first way, you sound nice; the second way, you're like an ogre.

Although the message gets across both ways, the word *please* makes it much nicer. And good manners build good relationships. Forgetting to use good manners can weaken and sometimes even fracture relationships. Failure to use polite words may cause others to attribute negative characteristics to you. Your social life could suffer because of manner violations.

Thank You

When someone does something nice for you, remember to say "thanks." It only takes a moment but it will improve your social relationships. People will view you as thoughtful and considerate. Even with simple things like someone holding a door open for you, or helping you with your packages—take the time to thank them.

When you receive something you like, it's important to acknowledge both the gift and your appreciation of the person who gave you the gift. That's good manners. You might feel that the words *thank you* aren't necessary if the person already knows that you like the gift. But people like to be told anyway. If you don't follow the social rules by saying "thank you," people may assume you don't like the gift. As a result, they may stop giving you gifts—even more importantly, they may consider you rude and stop hanging around with you.

Sending thank-you notes is also a good idea, especially if you received the gift through the mail. Even if you already told the person *thank you*, it never hurts to also send a note as

115

well. Most people appreciate the extra step. This can also enhance your social image.

It can be confusing to receive a number of gifts at the same time, say, at a birthday party or shower. You can easily forget who gave what unless you ask someone to help you keep track. With someone else making a list, you can easily send thank-you notes.

Receiving something you don't like, is a lot harder to deal with, and requires tact and discretion. On the one hand, you don't have to lie about the gift, professing how much you like it. But if you don't show appreciation, you'll hurt the giver's feelings.

"This is awful! What were you thinking?" may be the words going through your mind. Remember that not every thought needs to be spoken. Many thoughts need to be filtered, rephrased or repackaged. Find creative ways to show appreciation for something that you dislike with carefully chosen words. "Thank you for thinking of me. I really appreciate your thoughtfulness" or "What a unique gift." "I imagine you spent a lot of time making this for me. Thanks for being so thoughtful." The old adage says, "It's the thought that counts," and when you get an absolutely hideous gift, that's what you'll need to focus on. Whether or not you treasure the gift, you can still treasure the giving of it. Besides, you may be able to return it later. If the gift can't be exchanged—if it's handmade or bought far away—there's little point in saying you don't like it anyway.

When the giver is very close to you you may be able to be completely honest about your reaction to an unwanted gift. But still try to be tactful. "Thanks for thinking of me. I do need a tie but I already have several blue ones. I don't want to hurt your feelings, but I'd like to exchange it for a similar one in black. Would you like to come with me to pick out *an-*

other one?" This way you can show appreciation while expressing your feelings.

Remember, it's the relationship that's important, not the gift. Look past the specific item and use the situation as a way to deepen the relationship.

You're Welcome

When someone else thanks you, respond by saying, "You're welcome." It basically means, "Thanks for saying thanks." This might seem like an unnecessary social ritual, but these are the social rules by which we live.

Some feel awkward being thanked and may shrug it off, saying, "Oh, it was nothing." But this can make the person offering the thanks feel awkward. It *was* something, and they're showing appreciation. Don't argue; accept it. Just say *you're welcome,* and you'll be demonstrating good manners.

Receiving Compliments

Accepting compliments can be difficult, especially if you have self-esteem difficulties. Sometimes people go to great lengths to explain away a compliment.

Compliment: You did a great job with that presentation.
Reply: No, anyone could have done that.

Compliment: That dress looks great on you.
Reply: This old thing?

When you do this, you reduce their chances of receiving a compliment in the future. Just say "Thank you." You might

117

add, "It's kind of you to say that," or something like that. But don't argue. The complimenter is trying to make you feel good about yourself or something you've done. Allow them to do that for you.

On the other hand, you don't want to respond to a compliment by saying, "I know." Then you'll appear to be conceited. Humbly accept their kind words.

Giving Compliments

People love to receive sincere compliments, and they like to be around people who say nice things to them. So if you develop a habit of complimenting others, may improve your social standing. Try it! See what happens.

Although any compliment is good, the best compliments involve character traits rather than appearance. For example:

You are so thoughtful! (character)

I really appreciate your integrity. Not too many people would stand up for that issue the way you do. (character)

These are both better than:

Nice hair! (appearance)

That outfit looks great on you! (appearance)

However, if you offer compliments constantly and for little reason, people will quickly catch on that you're insincere.

What if someone shows up with a horrendous haircut and asks you what you think? Or you attend a play they're in and their performance is poor? This would be similar to the situation when you get a gift you don't like. Be tactful. Remember: the person is more important than your complete, unfiltered opinion. You might say, "I can tell you really worked hard on that play." You don't have to lie, but be careful how you express the truth.

I'm Sorry

This is a statement we don't hear enough—*I'm sorry*. It's good manners to apologize when you make a mistake or inconvenience someone. If you arrive late, for example, and have kept someone waiting, it would be considered rude and inconsiderate to not apologize for making the other person wait. This shows that you value and respect the other person and their time.

AD/HD provides more than ample opportunities to offer apologies. There can be forgotten items or tasks, late arrivals, and sometimes annoying behaviors. As the previous chapters have described, these behaviors can damage your relationships. But an apology goes a long way to bridge the gap, repairing and building relationships.

Some feel it's a sign of weakness to apologize—that an apology is like admitting defeat. Not at all! That attitude comes from a false sense of pride. An apology means that you take responsibility for your actions. It actually takes a mature person to offer a sincere apology.

It's amazing how easily people accept an apology—*as long as it's accompanied by a commitment to try to change the offending behavior.* If your apology is no more than empty words, that will often anger others. They'll feel used. But if you honestly feel bad about what you've done, and promise to work hard at improving your behavior, you'll usually find acceptance.

119

That's Okay

When others offer an apology, it is important to graciously accept it. Social relationships are *reciprocal*—they involve give and take. There will be plenty of times when you'll need someone to accept your apology.

It's important for you to move beyond the incident. Forgive the behavior. Let it go. Some people keep bringing up events that happened 110 years ago. Grudge-holding is not productive, and it's *counter*-productive if you want an ongoing relationship with that person. Accept apologies and move on.

The Wrong Way to Deal with an Apology

Apology: I'm sorry I was late.

Reply: *You should be! I was waiting 37 minutes for you!*

Apology: I'm really sorry, I'll try real hard not to be late again.

Reply: *Yeah, I hear you, but that doesn't get me my 37 minutes back. There are other things I could have been doing, you know. In fact, this is the 14th time you have been late in the past five years. I've been counting.*

As you can clearly see, this does nothing to move the relationship forward. In fact, it actually pulls the people apart.

A Better Way to Deal with an Apology

Apology: I'm sorry I was late.

120

Reply: *That's okay, I was able to read some*
           of my book while I was waiting.

Apology: *Thanks for being so understanding. I*
           really appreciate that!

As you can see, this does move the relationship forward. It's good manners to demonstrate compassion and understanding.

An Advanced Way to Deal with an Apology

If the offending behavior is really troubling you, you may need to discuss the behavior instead of dismissing it quickly with a *that's okay.* But do this in a sensitive, diplomatic manner. Your goal is to not only to express your honest feelings about the behavior, but also to establish good ground rules for the advancement of the relationship.

Apology: *I'm sorry I was late.*

Reply: *You know John, I like you and I want to spend*
           time with you. But I do feel that it's important
           to our relationship to let you know that I do
           find your lateness to be a problem. I really
           wish that we can work together to find some
           way to have this not be an problem for us.

Apology: *You know, you're right. I really am sorry, and*
           I know that this isn't the first time I have kept
           you waiting. I'm wondering if I were to call
           you before I really left, if that would be better.
           That way you wouldn't wait for me if I got a
           late start.

121

Reply: *That's a good idea. Let's try it next time. Now where are we supposed to be going?*

And so the relationship moves forward.

Introducing Yourself

At parties, in church, at conferences, on trips, at work, or just out with friends, you may find yourself with people you don't know. You may see certain people you'd *like* to know. Or you may be thrown together in work or social situations with people you *need* to know. Some people are hesitant to introduce themselves to someone new. If you want to expand your social relationships, introductions are a necessity.

QUICK TIP

Here's the formula for an introduction:
Your name + something simple (and short) about your self = Introduction

"Hi, I'm Ray. I work in accounting. Who are you?"

Often you don't even have to ask, "Who are you?" The other person may just respond with their name. After these basics, follow up with a question related to the mutual event.

Have you ever been to one of these before?
How long have you known Sam?

Most people are happy to meet new people. Some may be too shy to approach you, but might greatly appreciate you talking with them. (And if you're the shy one, you can wait and hope that someone approaches you.)

122

Pay attention to your surroundings. Are you in a situation where people expect to meet new people? Strangers in a common activity—at work or in volunteer efforts—are generally open to meeting people. In a professional context, this is called networking. In obviously social situations—bars, parties, church activities—meeting people is the whole idea.

If you want to meet someone in a neutral spot, such as a store, it's more difficult. Most people are reluctant to meet strangers in non-social environments. But you never know. Start with a smile, then a hello, then an introduction—and hope for the best. If the person doesn't respond, don't take it personally. Respect their privacy and drop the matter.

Introducing Others

Introductions serve as a way to bring strangers together. When you are with people who do not know each other, it is polite to introduce them. Otherwise people can feel awkward. A typical introduction might be:

"John, I'd like you to meet Mary. She and I are co-workers. John is an old friend from college."

There are rules about which person you name first, but don't worry about that right now. You can read up on it later in a manners book if you want. Just be considerate to both people, say both names clearly, and mention something about them. Ideally, you want to give them a conversation-starter.

"Mary's originally from England. John, didn't you take a trip there last year?"

And suddenly they're chatting like old friends about the best pubs in her homeland. You don't have to work too hard at forging a common link—they may do that themselves—but try to get at least one of them talking.

Because you have AD/HD, you may not always remember someone's name. What happens when you need to introduce someone, but you've forgotten their name? There are several tricks you could try:

(a) Admit privately to the one whose name you remember that you've forgotten the other one's name. Then you could say something like, "Oh this is an old college friend," and your other friend will jump in with a self-introduction.

(b) Say several things you do remember about the person, just "forgetting" to mention the name. Perhaps the people will trade names themselves and get you off the hook.

(c) Find someone else in the room and whisper, "Help me! I've just blanked out on that person's name!"

(d) Be honest. "Sorry. Brain freeze. I want to introduce you, but your name has escaped me. I have a terrible time remembering names. Please don't take it personally."

Greetings—Say *Hi*

It is customary to say *hi* or *hello* when you first see someone. *Hey, Good to see you,* or *Good morning* also work. In some way you need to acknowledge the person's presence. It's considered rude to walk into a room, see people, and say nothing. Once you have said *hi* to a person, that is usually good for the whole day. You don't need to keep saying *hi* each time you see a person, though a smile and nod are always nice.

When seeing someone you know at the mall or on the street, it is good manners to stop and say hello. At times you may be in such a rush that you don't want to stop. You might breeze right by a good friend because you're in a hurry. That would offend them. Good manners would dictate stopping to say hello, followed by a brief conversation. The brief conversation may be an explanation as to why you cannot stay and talk longer, but it is important to acknowledge the person. If you explain that you're busy, the person will know that you'd *like* to talk but you *can't*. And so good feelings will be maintained.

Maybe you have time to talk, but the other person's in a hurry. If you start rambling on and on, your friend may be in a difficult spot—wanting to be polite, but not having the time to chat. If you're unsure, just ask. "Am I keeping you from anything?"

Physical Contact when saying *Hi*

The rules about physical greetings are dictated by the culture—whether a national culture, business culture, or family culture. So be aware of your surroundings. Watch others as they greet people. What's acceptable in your business, in your social circle, in your family?

Men generally shake hands when they greet someone. Women may shake hands when they meet in a business situation, but not usually in a social situation unless it is a formal event. Women may hug close friends when greeting them, but men usually don't—at least not in the United States. Among family members, kisses and hugs are often appropriate.

Always be careful with male-female greetings, since these can have an unintended sexual element. When in doubt, choose the less physical greeting. Handshakes are always pretty safe.

Saying *Goodbye*

It is also necessary, according to the rules of proper etiquette, to say *goodbye* when you're leaving or someone is leaving you. *See ya later* and even *Later* also work. These phrases bring official closure to your time together.

Sometimes you might just get up and leave when you get bored or feel that it's time to go. Others may spend a great deal of time looking for you, because no one knew that you left. Your quick departure may be misinterpreted.

Phone Manners

Greetings. Yes, there are also proper ways to answer and speak on the telephone. It would be inappropriate, for example, to answer the phone saying, "Yo," "Yeah," or "What do you want?" Be attentive and respectful when answering the telephone. A simple *Hi* or *Hello* will do. Some people go further and say, "Hello, this is so-and-so, Can I help you?" Find a pleasant greeting that works for you.

Messages. If the call is not for you, it's good manners to offer to take a message. Since you may forget some of the details, be sure to write the information down. Ask the caller for their name, phone number, a brief message, and when the call can be returned. Then it's equally important to make sure the message gets to the intended person. There is nothing more frustrating than to have someone *take* a message and then not *give* it to you.

If you have difficulty taking messages or giving messages to the intended person, it would be better to have the person call back and leave a message on the answering machine. If an answering machine is not available, then just ask the person to call back later. That way the person won't think that a message was delivered when it wasn't.

Solicitors. It's okay to hang up on unsolicited sales calls. Since the telemarketers usually don't stop talking, you will need to interrupt them and say, "Sorry I'm not interested." Then hang up.

Don't stay on the line or they will just start talking to you about why you should be interested. (They're trained to try to overcome your objections.) Especially since you may have difficulty with impulsive purchases, a conversation with a telephone solicitor is definitely not desirable. To avoid temptation, get off the phone as quickly as possible.

Call Waiting. Call waiting presents some interesting manner dilemmas. In general, it's considered rude to interrupt one conversation to start another. Yet on the phone, this seems to be somewhat acceptable.

If you have call waiting, it's best to ignore the beep unless you're expecting an important call. If you do need to check the incoming call, excuse yourself politely from the current call with a brief word of explanation. "I hate to interrupt you, but I'm expecting a call from my doctor, I hope you don't mind me checking."

Call waiting is a challenge for anyone, but especially for those with AD/HD. You're forced to make split-second decisions about the importance of different calls—and it's easy to offend someone in the process. It's best to let the

127

phone beep unless you know there's an important reason to pick up the second call.

Eating

Dining in someone else's home. When invited to someone's house for a meal, it's always a good idea to bring something along as a token of appreciation. A dish of food, wine, or a plant or candle would be fitting—anything that says, *I appreciate you having me over.*

There are proper ways to conduct yourself once you arrive at someone else's home. Before you even sit down at the table, observe what other people in the room are doing—especially the host or hostess. Do they have their shoes on or off? Are they sitting in the family room talking, or are people already being seated at the table? It's always nice to offer to help.

Once you actually make it to the dinner table, you should be aware of some other rules of etiquette. Always wait for the host or hostess to be seated. Then await their instructions before you begin to eat. Usually they will tell you that it's time to eat, they may pray, or the host/hostess will pick up their utensils and begin to eat. Those are all signs that you too can begin to eat. It is considered very rude to begin eating before the host or hostess.

If you violate the rules of etiquette, you may not be asked to return. Everything your mother ever told you still applies:
- Chew with your mouth closed.
- Don't talk with your mouth full.
- Ask to have items passed to you rather than reaching.
- Use your napkin.
- Keep your elbows off the table.
- When finished, ask to be excused from the table.

If someone addresses you while you have a mouthful of food, just give him or her a look that acknowledges their inquiry but do not begin talking while you are still chewing. This can be hard for you because of your struggle with impatience. You may be antsy, but it is important to wait to speak. There's not too much that's worth saying with a mouth full of food.

Avoid reaching across the table for something you need. Instead, kindly ask the closest person to hand it to you. A statement such as *"Please pass the mashed potatoes"* gets the job done with proper manners.

Now, what to do with all those forks? Simply start from the outside and work your way in with each course. If you're not sure how to eat something, or which utensil to use, just wait and watch others.

When you're invited for a meal, it's a social occasion. That means it's not just about food—it's about *relationships*. So it would be impolite to "eat and run," that is, to leave quickly after the meal is finished. After eating it's customary to sit and talk for a while.

Hosting a meal in your home. All the social rules mentioned above also apply when you have guests over in your own home. However, being a host carries some added responsibilities.

You need to meet and greet your guests and help them to feel comfortable in your home. Make sure to go to the door to meet your guests. Even if they are able to let themselves in, it's still polite to meet them as soon as they come to your house.

Warmly greet arriving guests. For example, say: "Hello, how are you?", "It is nice to see you!", or "I'm glad you could come." These are all great ways to welcome guests into your home. If they're wearing coats, offer to take them.

Offer to get your guests something to drink or eat. Show your guests where to go and sit.

Remember to include your guests in conversations and activities. Don't leave your guests to finish writing bills or folding the laundry. Even if you have a great idea or just remember something you've forgotten, please wait until your guests have departed. It is considered very rude to leave your guests and wander off, tending to your normal routine activities without them. If the phone rings, ignore it, or explain quickly to the caller that you're busy and will have to call back. Better yet, turn off the ringer and let your answering machine take the calls.

Jim was so distracted when others came to see him that he often retreated to the quiet of another room. He was fearful of making social errors, so he thought it would be best to watch TV on his own. But his guests felt abandoned. They almost never came back. They had come to spend time with Jim, not with his television.

As a host or hostess, you will also need to walk your guests to the door when it's time to leave—even if they are able to let themselves out. Thank them for coming and say *goodbye*. Try to be aware of when people are preparing to leave. They are being polite by coming to you and saying goodbye. It would be impolite of you to ignore them, to continue talking with others or tending to some activity. When someone lets you know they need to leave, be sure to:

- Stop what you're doing.
- Get their coat, if they had one.
- Walk them to the door.
- Thank them for coming and say goodbye.

Taking Turns and Waiting

It's good manners to take turns. It may be hard for you to wait in line or to wait for your turn. If you're engaged in a taking-turns activity such as a video game or card game, you may forget to let the other person have a turn. If this happens, the other person will begin to feel left out and probably won't want to socialize with you again.

This can also happen in conversations if you forget to give others the opportunity to talk. Practice putting pauses in your speech, just so others can respond. On the other hand, if you have AD/HD without hyperactivity you may be so over-whelmed at social encounters that you may not speak much at all. You would benefit from learning to take your turn in conversations.

Offering and Asking for Help

People who are helpful are generally liked by others. Be on the lookout for opportunities to be helpful. Often people don't ask directly for help—instead they drop hints. Learn to read these hints, and be ready to offer a lift or a listening ear.

Imagine a co-worker saying something like this: "Are you planning to be at work this Thursday? Me, too. We've got that big meeting. Unfortunately, I've got to take my car to the shop. It's that mechanic only a couple of blocks from where you live. It's right on your way to work, right? Well, I'll be dropping it off in the morning. I don't know, maybe I'll grab a bus or something. I'm not too familiar with that area. What do you suggest?"

Your co-worker is asking you for a ride—not coming right out and requesting it, but presenting a need and allow-

131

ing you to offer to meet it. If you *don't* offer to help, your co-worker will think you're unkind, not realizing that you don't even realize you've been asked for help. There are a million different subtleties like this in everyday conversation which require you to respond with good manners. (Well maybe not a million, but sometimes it feels that way.)

Asking for help is a social skill many are lacking and not just people with AD/HD. However, research has shown that children with learning disabilities, including AD/HD, don't ask for help as much as other children. [4] Although this can help them develop self-sufficiency, they often get frustrated and overwhelmed. It also robs them of social relationships with those who would help them.

Obviously you don't want to ask for help all the time, but life involves give and take. You help others sometimes, and others help you. There's nothing wrong with asking for assistance when you need it.

Ask for help directly because others may miss your hints (just as you have probably missed hints that others have dropped you.) Direct communication is best.

My car's in the shop. Could you drive me to work tomorrow? I'd appreciate it. That's a request for help. No one will mind being asked like that, even if they can't help you.

Summary

This chapter covers just a few of the manners which can be difficult for those with AD/HD. There are many more. I discuss some other conversational manners in the communication chapter.

If you want more information on manners, your local bookstore or library should have several books on the subject. You might also consult newspaper columns such as "Miss

Manners" or "Ms. Demeanor." These resources will offer you more details than you'll ever want to know. I'd suggest that you practice a few new manners at a time, while keeping in mind the general idea of just plain being nice. Remember, think about how you like to be treated, then treat others that way.

JUST THE FACTS

- Manners are basically rules of niceness.

- Since people with AD/HD often have difficulties with inattention, hyperactivity, and impulsivity, they may have a more difficult time picking up these social rules.

- If you lack manners, others may interpret your actions as thoughtless or selfish, even though you have the good intentions.

- Not every thought needs to be spoken. Diplomacy is often needed.

- **Please.** Saying please turns commands into requests.

- **Thanks:** When someone gives you something, it is important to acknowledge both the gift and your appreciation of the person who gave you the gift. There are creative ways to show appreciation with discretion for something that you dislike.

133

- **You're welcome.** It basically means, *thanks for saying thanks*.

- **Giving and receiving compliments.** Find honest reasons to compliment those around you. People love to receive compliments. The best compliments involve character traits rather than appearance.

- **I'm sorry.** It's good manners to apologize when you make a mistake or inconvenience someone—but you'll need to follow up with attempts to change the offending behavior.

- **That's okay.** When others apologize, it's important to graciously accept their apology. Social relationships are reciprocal—they involve give and take.

- **Introductions** serve as a way to bring strangers together.

- **Greetings.** Say *hi* or *hello* when you first see someone to acknowledge their presence. It's considered rude to walk into a room, see people, and say nothing.

- **Goodbye.** Let people know when you're leaving. Don't just walk out.

- **Phone manners.** Use a pleasant greeting. Offer to take a message for someone who's not there, save call waiting for urgent calls you expect.

- **Eating Etiquette**.
  - Don't begin eating before the host or hostess.
  - Chew with your mouth closed.
  - Don't talk with your mouth full.
  - Ask to have items passed to you rather than reaching.
  - Use your napkin.
  - Keep your elbows off the table.
  - When finished, ask to be excused from the table.

- **Hosting**: Meet, greet, include people in conversation, and say goodbye.

- Meals with others are more about relationships than food.

NOTES

1. Mitchell, M. (1999, May 23). Ms. Demeanor Column. *Philadelphia Inquirer*.
2. Lavoie, R. (1994). *Learning disabilities and social skills:last one picked,...first one picked on.* Washinton, D.C.: WETA - TV

Chapter 8

Are You Listening?
—Communication Skills:
Verbal and Non-verbal

THROUGHOUT HISTORY, PEOPLE have made efforts to communicate with each other—from pictures drawn on cave walls to smoke signals to cell phones. While technology has made huge advances in finding *methods* of communication, we still seem to be lagging behind in knowing *how* to communicate effectively. Nowadays you can pick up the phone and talk with someone in Europe and at the same time e-mail someone in Australia, but technology hasn't helped us know *what* to say.

Like any other social interaction, communication has rules. If you want your conversations to be considered socially appropriate, you need to be aware of the guidelines. These basically fall into two categories:

Verbal Communication –things you or someone else says

Non-Verbal Communication—things you or someone else does

Verbal Communication

Talking is easy, right? But *conversing* may be a challenge for you. How do you start a conversation, listen well, ask ques-

137

tions, show others you're listening, speak appropriately, and end a conversation? These are all crucial components to effective communication.

For some people, it seems effortless. You may know some folks who can talk about anything in a way that others enjoy. But many with AD/HD find it awkward to start and maintain good conversations. This is often because they lack certain skills. Maybe that's your situation. Maybe you talk well but don't listen. Maybe you start conversations but don't know how to end them. You might be like the baseball player who slams every fastball he sees, but can't hit the curve. You need to develop your total game. So let's take a look at each of these components of effective verbal communication.

Joining a Conversation

Have you ever played Double Dutch with a jump rope? Joining a conversation is something like trying to hop in while the rope is turning. Before you make your move, you have to be aware of a number of factors and make certain assessments. If you don't, the conversation (like the jump rope) may stop short.

For instance, it's considered rude to jump into a conversation and begin asking questions that the others have already heard the answers to. This seems self-centered. Think about it for a minute. Why should the entire conversation stop and everyone one else wait while you get caught up?

It's also best to listen to the conversation for a bit before jumping in. Try to understand what they're talking about so you don't disrupt the flow of the conversation.

And make sure it's okay for you to join in. If two people are sitting at a table talking, don't just plop yourself next to them. Ask if it's okay to join them. It might be a private conversation. The same is true if several people are standing around talking. Before you jump in, try to determine whether it's an *exclusive* or *inclusive* conversation. Will you be welcome? When in doubt, ask—"Is it okay to join you?"

Listening by Reflecting Content

Listening seems to be a lost art. And not just for those with AD/HD. The world seems full of talkers and short on listeners. If you are able to develop good listening skills, your social interactions should dramatically improve. People often seek out others who listen. (That's one reason that professional counselors are in such demand.)

However, listening is an acquired skill. Most of us don't just naturally listen. In fact, in the graduate counseling program where I teach, we spend a lot of time teaching students just how to listen effectively. It takes some practice.

Listening has two basic parts. When you listen effectively:

- You are able to understand the *content* of what the person has said.

- You are able to understand the *person's feelings*.

People want to know that a listener is understanding what they're saying. Therefore, good listening involves *reflecting*. Think of yourself as a mirror, sending back an image of the person's statements. Let's call this the "echo approach."

First, you need to echo back the *content* of the story or situation they're talking about. As you understand the facts they're giving you, repeat them back in the same or slightly different words.

Other Person:	*I just lost my job! I can't believe they fired me today.*
You:	*Oh no. You lost your job today?*

On the surface, it may seem unnecessary. Why do you have to repeat the information? The person needs to know that you've received the information—that you're getting it— and this is the way to tell them. It allows you both to clarify the facts. And it makes the other person feel *heard*.

EXERCISE

Reflection of Content - The Echo:

1. At least five times during a conversation, try to re- flect back—echo—the content of what you have heard.

2. Then watch what happens to the conversation. The person should continue talking, giving you more information.

3. You may want to ask someone to practice this with you. Ask them to tell you when you are echoing properly and when you are misinterpreting what they have said. (People will probably do this naturally in a conversation, but it never hurts to practice with someone who is trying to help you.)

The echo approach is especially important for those with AD/HD. Because of the blinks and blanks in your atten- tion, it is easy to miss certain details. Reflection of the con- tent allows you to double-check what you think you've heard.

Whenever anyone gives you an instruction—a boss, your spouse, or a stranger giving you directions—*always repeat the instructions back.* People won't mind this extra step. In fact, they'll probably appreciate the fact that you care enough to get it right.

Follow this up by asking if there is anything else.

So you need the report by tomorrow morning. Is that right? Is there anything else?

So that's milk, eggs, bread, and a newspaper. Anything else, hon?

Turn left at the Exxon station, three lights and right on Baker Avenue, and it'll be the big, red house on the left. Is that right? Did I get it all?

TIPS FOR THOSE WITHOUT AD/HD

1. If you're talking with someone who has AD/HD, ask them to repeat back what they heard you say. If you've given important directions, you want to make sure they've heard the entire message.

   Before you go, please tell me what you heard me ask you to do.

2. This approach takes less than one minute and can reduce the incredible amount of stress, conflict and misunderstandings in a relationship where the blinks and blanks of AD/HD are a problem.

Listening by Reflecting Feelings

Besides reflecting the content of what people say, you should also try to understand their *feelings*. Effective communication involves both information and emotion. The emotion is just as important as the content, sometimes even more so. When someone people tell you a story, they have a reason for sharing this with you. They may be happy, sad or angry. They want to communicate their feelings to you.

Other Person:	*I just lost my job! I can't believe they fired me today.*
You:	*You seem really upset!*

The echo approach works here, too, but this time you're reflecting feelings rather than facts. This takes a little more perception. Most people give off pretty obvious clues about their feelings. If you're unsure of their emotions, you can always ask, "How do you feel about that?"

Stay away from judgments here. You don't need to comment on whether their feelings are "right" or "wrong." Just echo back how they seem to be feeling.

EXERCISE

Finding Feelings

1. Make a list of all the feeling words that you can think of. Make sure they are indeed feelings and not thoughts or actions. People often get thoughts and feelings confused. Feeling terms are usually only one word, not phrases.

142

2. Refer to your list to help you become aware of the feelings of others.

3. Keep adding feeling words to your list.

Reflection of Feelings
1. At least five times during a conversation, try to reflect back only the feelings you have heard.
2. Watch what happens to the conversation. The person should continue talking, this time telling you more about how they feel.
3. You may want to ask someone to practice this with you, to give you feedback on when you are hearing it right and when you are misinterpreting what they've said.

To become an effective listener, you need to understand both the *content* and the *feelings* being conveyed. People will appreciate you as a listener when you let them know you're getting both what they're saying and what they're feeling.

Other Person: *I just lost my job! I can't believe that they fired me today.*

You: *You seem to be feeling upset because you lost your job today.*

EXERCISE

Reflecting Feeling + Content

1. Here's one trick to help you as you reflect both con-
    tent and feelings. Try putting your response into
    one of the following formulas: *You seem to be feel-
    ing* _____ *because* _____.
    I'm wondering if you are feeling _____ *because*
    _____.

2. You can vary the words or the order, but somehow
    mention both feelings and facts. You might even
    want to practice saying each half separately until
    you can get the hang of putting them together. It
    may help you to look for the *because* link.

3. Although it will sound awkward at first, try using
    the formula at least five times in a conversation.
    Watch to see how the person responds to your state-
    ments. You should be pleasantly surprised with the
    results.

Minimal Encouragers

Eavesdrop on a conversation sometime—perhaps in a
crowded restaurant or mall. Pay special attention to people
as they're listening. Chances are, you'll see them nod every
so often in agreement.

These may seem unnecessary, but they're actually quite
important for effective communication. Those little responses
are actually saying, "Keep going. I'm listening. This is interesting." They are called "minimal encouragers" because they

offer gentle support to the person talking. Without them, the people might fear that they're boring their listeners, or they've lost them.

Verbal encouragers are especially important in phone conversations, because there is no visual feedback. For all you know, the listener might have left the room to make a sandwich—unless you keep hearing those encouragers. "Mmm-hmm. . . . Gotcha. . . . Absolutely."

Try using minimal encouragers and head nods in your next conversation to let the person know you're listening. If you have trouble talking too much, limit yourself to these minimal responses. That will help keep the focus on the other person.

Questions

When you are first getting to know someone, the majority of your initial communication will probably consist of questions and answers. It is usually through questions that you get to know about someone, and their interests.

Questions also show your interest in what the other person is saying—as long as they are questions about what is being said. If the person is talking about the weather, don't ask about the stock market. But you can deepen a conversation (and a relationship) by asking good questions.

There are different types of questions and some are better than others.

Open questions are usually better than **closed questions.** A closed question can be answered in a few words (or less). They usually close the door on any continued conversation.

Tom: *I'm really upset about my girlfriend
        breaking up with me last night.*

145

Mark: *So, where were you when she told you?*
         (closed question)

Tom: *Michelangelo's.*

Tom might still continue talking, but Mark's question isn't helping to move the conversation.

Open questions, on the other hand, encourage the other person to keep talking. They hold the door open for more conversation.

Tom: *I'm really upset about my girlfriend breaking up with me last night.*

Mark: *So what happened? (open question)*

Tom: *We had been together for three years. I thought this was going to be the one. And now look what happened. I didn't even see it coming.*

This open question encourages Tom to tell more. Whenever possible, use open questions to keep conversations moving along.

There are also what I call **naked questions.** These are questions that ask for more information, but they don't reflect any of the facts or feelings of the previous statements. They're not all bad. They can show the talker that you're interested in the subject and want to know more, but they don't make the strongest connection. We already discussed how much people appreciate reflective listening. Naked questions pass up the opportunity to reflect what a person's saying. The conversation seems more like an interview. Information is requested and supplied, but the personal connection may be limited.

Tom: *I'm really upset about my girlfriend breaking up with me last night.*

Mark: *So, what happened?*

Although Mark's question isn't bad, it fails to address Tom's feelings. Mark would be a better friend by reflecting the emotions Tom is expressing.

Let's try the dialogue again, but this time we'll have Mark address Tom's feelings and content first, before asking his questions.

Tom: *I'm really upset about my girlfriend breaking up with me last night.*

Mark: *Yeah, you seem real upset that your girlfriend broke up with you. So, what happened?*

Now Mark is letting Tom know that he's connecting with him. The question moves the conversation forward, but the reflective statements show support. It's not just an interview; it's a heart-to-heart talk.

It's always good to ask questions, rather than dominating the conversation. Questions indicate interest in the other person and the subject matter. But as you get more accustomed to asking questions, steer yourself toward open questions rather than closed ones and start "dressing" those naked questions in reflective statements.

147

Tracking

Due to random thoughts and tangential relationships, it's common for a person with AD/HD to change the topic of conversation suddenly, or so it may seem. Sometimes you see a connection between the two subjects, but no one else does. People think you are not listening and are launching into a whole new direction, when that's not really the case. Still, according to attribution theory, when people can't see the connection, they'll attribute your "off-the-wall" comments to a lack of listening.

You can pull a conversation back by explaining the links in your own mind. So if you find yourself going off on what appear to others as tangents, be sure to explain how the thoughts are connected in your mind. This will help others view you as a good listener.

You may also have a desire to talk about yourself. It's natural for people to connect what others are saying with their own experiences, but be sure to find a balance. People aren't always interested in your stories. Make sure your conversation includes their thoughts and ideas as well as your own. If you're only talking about yourself, you'll soon find yourself alone.

TIPS FOR STAYING ON TRACK

1. Make sure that what you say is responding to what someone has just said.

2. Make sure the person is finished before you change the topic. If you begin talking about yourself and your experiences with the topic, make sure the other person has enough of an opportunity to tell his or her own story too.

Stopping

When a conversation is ending, be sure to use appropriate social exit comments. You might expect that people would just leave when they're done talking. But politeness requires that people ease out of conversations. Listen to others as they end conversations. Sometimes they string together three or four exit comments before finally leaving.

Well, it was great to see you.
You, too.
I've gotta get going.
Yeah, I should be moving along, too.
Catch you later.
Okay.
Goodbye.
Bye.

You don't always have to go through all that. The idea is, you don't want to give the impression: "I'm tiring of talking with you, so I'm outta here" (even if that's true). If you abruptly exit conversations when you have nothing more to say, you can frustrate and insult others. They may wonder what just happened. Did they offend you? Did you leave in a huff? Were you ill? Was there an emergency? People will jump to all sorts of inaccurate conclusions when you don't follow the social rules of stopping conversations. To avoid this, ease into your departure.

"It's been nice talking with you. Until next time. See ya. Gotta go." There are lots of ways to say goodbye. Pick two or three of them. Whatever works for you will probably be fine. It takes only about five seconds to ease out of a conversation gracefully, but it's five seconds well spent!

149

Communication Roadblocks

You may be so focused on *what* you're saying that you may not pay attention to *how* you're saying it. Any of these errors can block the development of interpersonal relationships.

Volume. Some people talk too loudly for the setting. In church, for instance, you usually need to talk softly. At a football stadium, you'll have to talk loudly. The mood is hushed at a classical music concert and boisterous at a rock concert. In some settings—parties or restaurants—you may need to continually adjust your volume according to the surrounding sound.

Speed. Some with AD/HD and hyperactivity become so excited about what they want to say that they talk way too fast for others to understand. Don't focus only on the ideas swirling around in your head; pay attention to your listeners. Are they following you? If not, slow down. They may not be able to listen as fast as you speak.

"Motor Mouth" was Maria's nickname. Unfortunately, most of her friends and family couldn't keep up with her rapid-fire thoughts. Although they loved the excitement and rush of ideas, they often became exhausted by the torrent of her words.

Fortunately, Maria had asked her friends to just let her know when she was speaking too quickly. She didn't always know when her rate increased, so she welcomed the prompts from her friends. That way, her friends could absorb her thoughts better and Maria could share her ideas with her friends in a manner that did not alienate them.

On the road, motorists can be unaware that they're picking up speed if they don't check the speedometer. In the same way, talkers can pick up speed without realizing it, especially if they're passionate about their subject. But listeners may feel assaulted by a barrage of fast-flying words. That makes it hard work to attend to what you're saying. So, chances are, your close friends would be more than willing to play traffic cop for you, if you ask them, to let you know when your conversation is "speeding."

Interruptions. You may have a hard time holding back thoughts. If you think it, you want to say it—even if someone else is talking. Of course this is rude to the speaker and disruptive to the conversation. So it's important to ask yourself how important the comment is and whether it's worth losing friends over. Probably not. Jot down your thought to talk about after the other person has finished.

Too Quiet. Some with AD/HD have the opposite problem. Overwhelmed by conversations and social noise, you may shut down and not enter into conversations. Missing pieces of information, because of your blinks and blanks, you find it easier to avoid saying anything. Unfortunately, if you don't talk, others never get to know you.

No doubt about it, conversation is risky business. You never know when you might do or say something wrong. That's why it's important to start small. Gather a group of good friends or family members around you and let them know about your AD/HD. (You could give them this book.) Ask them in advance to help you. With their support, you can begin taking chances in conversation. You'll probably make some of these conversational errors, but the best way to learn to talk more effectively is to practice talking. Try to set yourself up for success by finding supportive people with whom you can practice your communication skills.

Ordering, Commanding Others

Most people have a difficult time when being ordered to do something. "You must . . ." or "Don't do it that way!" Sometimes in the economy of words, those with AD/HD forget to enlist support for their idea and cut right to the point on their mind, "Do this now!" Enlisting cooperation is much better than barking orders.

Fixing, Judging, and Minimizing

Some people love to fix things. The VCR goes on the fritz and they pry it open and poke around with a screw driver, whether they know what they're doing or not. Some people also like to fix other people's problems. but this is dangerous territory.

As your friends share their problems, you may have a strong impulse to tell them what to do. Fight it. You see, advice rarely helps, especially when it hasn't been asked for. When you give unsolicited advice, you are implying, "You, poor wretch, have no way of climbing out of your predicament. But I, the enlightened one, will give you all the answers you need." Well, maybe not in so many words, but it can feel like that.

Even professional counselors are instructed not to give advice. Instead they are trained to help people find their own solutions. It's generally much more helpful to listen to the person, making statements or asking questions along the way, rather than trying to tell someone what they should do. That way, you can help the person come to understand what they want to do.

Judging the behavior of someone else rarely earns you social points. If you criticize others, in most cases you won't be viewed as helpful. When you pass judgment, it seems as if you think you're better than the other person, even if you're just offering an opinion. Don't make comments like, "That's wrong." or "That was really stupid!" They do nothing to improve your social status.

Even positive comments like, "That's right." and "That's exactly what you should have done." are evaluative and judgemental. Work on being supportive rather than judgmental. If you think supportive thoughts about others, you'll be less tempted to blurt out harsh judgments.

Also be careful about **minimizing**. This usually comes from well-meaning people who are trying to cheer someone up. "Oh, that's not so bad. Tomorrow you'll forget all about it." Sure, they're trying to be nice, but they're totally dismissing the way the person is feeling right now. It's important to accept a person's feelings and empathize with them. Of course, you want to help them feel better, but first you need to support them.

Nonverbal Communication

In *"The Gambler,"* Kenny Rogers sang about body language. Reading people's faces is an important skill in poker. This gambler knew his fellow traveler was "out of aces" just by the way he held his hand.

But it's not just card-players who communicate without words. Everyone does. Skilled communicators learn how to read body language, and how to use it effectively. Yet this is often difficult for those with AD/HD. It's hard enough to focus on people's words, and reading nonverbal signals can be even tougher.

Your Body Language

Even when you're not saying anything, your body can communicate a lot about what you're thinking or feeling. In conversation, it's important to look like you're listening and interested in what the other person is saying. If you don't, people can become offended. They won't want to talk with you if they think you're not listening.

On the other hand, when your body language shows interest in the other person, they'll feel comfortable with you. They'll feel heard, cared for, valued. You're creating a safe place for them, providing hospitality, allowing them to confide in you. All of that will improve your social status immensely—and you haven't even said anything yet. Your physical presence alone can communicate your interest.

One counselor has identified five parts of good conversational body language.[1] You can remember them with the acronym OFFER, since you're *offering* your attention.

OFFER refers to the following body language components :

- **Open** posture
- **Face** the person squarely
- Lean **Forward**
- Make **Eye** contact
- **Relax**

Let's look at each of these components.

Open Posture

Comfortably keep your arms at your sides and your feet flat on the floor. If you cross your arms or legs, this often conveys the message that you are displeased, angry, or defensive. That stance closes you off from the other person. But an open stance—standing or seated—gives the signal that you're open to them and what they're saying.

Face Squarely

To communicate effectively with someone, sit or stand squarely facing them. This lets them know they have your full attention. It puts them fully in your field of vision, keeping distractions out of sight. Turn your chair if you need to, or turn your shoulders to face them directly.

Lean Forward

Leaning toward someone conveys interest in them and their message. Obviously leaning away would have the opposite impact. I'm talking about a very slight forward tilt, as if you were trying to hear better. Leaning backwards implies that you are not interested in the other person or what they are saying.

Eye Contact

In American culture, regular eye contact conveys that you want to hear what the other person has to say. (Note, however, that some other cultures discourage eye contact.) Steady eye contact is different from staring. You may look away now and then—in fact it's common for people to look up or down to gather thoughts and memories. But don't be looking around the room or up at the ceiling for more than about 25 percent of the time. That makes people feel disconnected from you.

You may need to ask others for feedback regarding your eye contact. Sometimes people don't realize how little eye contact they're actually making.

Jeremy approached me after a lecture on social skills and said he had lots of problems socializing. No one would go out with him on a date. He had asked a number of girls but never got an acceptance. He wondered what he was doing wrong.

As he talked with me, Jeremy never looked at me. He was looking at his shoes, around the room, or up at the ceiling. There might have been other social rules he was violating too, but I knew he definitely needed to work on improving his eye contact. Even though his conversational skills seemed fine, without eye contact it was difficult to talk with him.

Jeremy seemed surprised when I mentioned his lack of eye contact. He didn't realize he wasn't looking at me as we talked. As he left, he was happy that he had something concrete to work on!

Relaxed

Try not to fidget nervously, and don't be stiff and robot-like. Tension can show up as too much motion or too little. Take deep breaths and find a comfortable position. You don't want to look like it's uncomfortable to be with the other person.

157

EXERCISE

To Improve Your Body Language

1. Record yourself talking with someone.
2. Review the videotape and study your body language.
3. Check out your behavior with the OFFER list.
   - Did you keep an **O**pen posture?
   - Did you **F**ace the person squarely?
   - Did you lean **F**orward at times?
   - How was your **E**ye contact?
   - Did you look **R**elaxed?
4. You may also ask someone else to review your video with you for additional feedback.
5. Practice any areas that needed improvement.
6. Do this again, in a different setting or with a different person, until you feel successful with your body language.

Note: If a video camera is not available:

- You can ask someone to observe you as you talk with someone else. Tell them about OFFER and ask them to give you feedback on those points.

- You could also ask them to give you feedback on these points as you talk with them.

Understanding Other People's Body Language

Communication also involves learning to pick up signs while the other person is talking. Beyond the words you hear, study the person's nonverbal behaviors such as posture, facial expressions, movements, and tone of voice.

Often nonverbal behavior just confirms what a person is saying verbally. For example, if someone says, "I'm sad," while crying—that's a match. Because people don't always

158

say what they mean it's important to be on the alert for mis-matches. Nonverbal behavior will give you important clues about what a person is *really* thinking or feeling.

For example, you may be talking with someone at a party. They need to leave soon, so they want you to stop talking, but they won't tell you directly. Instead, they'll give you any number of signals. They might:

- begin looking at their watch or glancing at a clock;
- gather their personal belongings together;
- start edging toward the door;
- change body position. If they were sitting, they might stand up;
- show facial signs of frustration or tension and per-haps even a yawn;
- begin looking away from you frequently; or
- begin to tap a pencil or a foot, as they become more anxious.

These are all examples of nonverbal communication. If they don't work, you might hear statements like, "My, it's getting late! I have to get up at 6:30 tomorrow. It's been a wonderful evening." But nonverbal communication is usu-ally tried first. If you want to improve your communication skills, it's important to crack this nonverbal code.

EXERCISE
To Improve Reading Body Language
1. Video tape a television show.

2. Watch the show, or part of a show, without the sound. Just by watching the nonverbal

---

language, jot down on paper what you think is going on and how you think the characters feel for each scene.

3. Watch the show again, this time with the sound.
   - Check out your guesses with what actually was being said.
   - How well did you guess?
   - When you guessed wrong, go back and watch that section again.
   - Do you now see clues you didn't see before?
   - When you guessed right, what clues did you see?

4. Repeat this exercise several times, using different types of shows, until you feel successful in interpreting nonverbal language.

Gary came into counseling with a smile from ear to ear. "You seem very happy," I reflected.

"I just saw my wife get angry last night," he replied. "It was great."

I did a double-take. "You're happy because you saw your wife get angry?"

"Yes," he said proudly. "She got real angry and this time I saw it. Do you know that she first started tapping her foot? Then she started squeezing her hands together. Then her face started getting red. Then her face got real red. Her voice got louder. Then she turned, walked out and slammed the door. I never saw all the stuff before. I just thought she got mad out of nowhere and slammed the door. But she did a lot of stuff before the door slamming started. I just never noticed that before!"

JUST THE FACTS

Verbal Communication Skills (things you or some-one else *says*)

- Repeat instructions and check to see if you heard the entire instruction. Follow this up by asking if there is anything else.

- If you are communicating with someone with AD/HD, ask them to repeat any instructions back to you, to make sure they've heard the entire message.

- Verbal communication has a number of components to take into consideration: joining a conversation, listening reflectively, asking questions, use of minimal encouragers, tracking, ending conversations, and avoiding communication roadblocks.

- Communication roadblocks include voice volume, speed, interruptions, being too quiet, giving advice, judging, and minimizing.

- In conversation, learn to reflect both the content and feeling of what the other person says (the echo approach).

Nonverbal Communication Skills (things you orsome one else *does*)

- Your body often says a lot about what you're thinking or feeling.

- The important elements of body language are represented by the acronym **OFFER**:
  Open posture
  Face the person squarely
  Lean **forward**
  Make **eye** contact
  Relax

- Become aware of elements such as body language, posture, facial expressions, movements and tone of voice.

NOTES

1. Egan, G. (1998). *The skilled helper: A problem management approach to helping* (6th ed.). Pacific Grove, California: Brooks/Cole Publishing Company. p. 63-64.

Chapter 9

What's Going on Here?
Reading the Situation:
Subtext and Context

NOSEEUMS.

Some parts of the world are plagued with these tiny bugs that bite people. Unfortunately, because they're so small, people don't see them (hence the common name *no-see-um*). Still, people are regularly bitten by what they can't see.

Subtext is like that sometimes—especially for people with AD/HD. Subtext is the hidden meaning of conversations. It's what people are *really* talking about, even though they're not saying a word about it. It may seems as if nothing is there, but you can still get bitten.

The signals are almost imperceptible. A raised eyebrow. A tone of voice. A pause. If you're not tuned in, you can miss the fact that someone's telling a joke or delivering an insult or just being polite. People with AD/HD, whose attention spans tend to capture the broad sweeps of activity, may miss the tiny details. You may often find yourself a beat behind. Everyone's laughing at a joke you didn't get. Or you think someone's really interested in what you're saying when they're just being polite. In any case, you've been bitten by the "noseeums" of subtext.

163

In his video, *Last One Picked...First One Picked On,* Richard Lavoie, who specializes in working with children with learning disabilities, says that schools ought to teach the "hidden curriculum." [1] He uses this term to refer to the unwritten, unspoken rules of social interaction. Although schools tend to do a good job of teaching academics, he says, they often neglect social items such as whom to sit with at lunch, or even how to get lunch, where to go for help, how to avoid getting beaten up, etc. For schoolchildren, the result of violating the hidden curriculum is often isolation and rejection. It's not much different for adults.

The key to understanding this hidden curriculum is subtext. You have to learn to read between the lines. In the field of poetry or drama, students search the text for clues about how the poet or character is feeling. These unspoken feelings then become a subtext that gives meaning to the text.

The same thing happens in conversation. People aren't always clear, above board, and direct. For instance, boys (and men, too) often want to appear tough and rugged, so they won't admit when they're hurting physically or emotionally. But they'll hint at it. Their words will say, "I'm fine. I can handle it." But their tone of voice is saying, "Please comfort me."

That's subtext. A person may say one thing, but mean something else. What is said (the text) is often very different from what is really being communicated (the subtext). Folks with AD/HD have to work extra hard to pay attention to the subtext.

Why Does the Subtext Exist?

Why don't people say what they mean? Are they just pathological liars? A few may be, but most people are just following social convention. People often use subtext to be polite.

They don't want to hurt your feelings, so they don't directly say what they're thinking. And sometimes people are afraid of the consequences of telling you the truth.

Consider the story of the emperor's new clothes. Although everyone knew that the emperor didn't have any clothes on, no one wanted to look foolish and pay the consequences for telling the truth. Everyone pretended it was a great-looking outfit. They said, "You look great!" but you can bet they were rolling their eyes and smirking. Finally a child pointed out the clear, undiluted truth: There were no new clothes; the emperor was parading around naked.

The people were trying to be polite. As long as the emperor believed he was well-clothed, they didn't want to hurt his feelings by telling the truth. That might cost them their lives. But if the emperor was a bit better at reading the subtext—the stares, the whispers, the pauses—he could have spared himself some embarrassment. It took a child to turn the subtext into text.

Our social world is built on subtext. In the movie *Liar, Liar*, Jim Carrey's character was suddenly unable to tell lies. This produced some comic moments as he was forced to be brutally honest in even the most innocent situations. What made it funny was that all of us can relate. We often don't say what we're actually thinking. When a friend asks, "How do I look?" we don't say, "Fat!"—even if that's the truth.

Let's say Suzy is performing with a community theater, and she invites her Aunt Rose to come and see her. Rose is also an actress, having appeared in some professional pro-

ductions, so her opinion is important to Suzy. Afterward, Suzy asks her aunt, "So what did you think?"

Rose looks up a moment to gather her thoughts and then says slowly, "It was very nice, Suzy. You certainly put a lot of work into that play, and there were some wonderful moments that touched my heart. It's a great play, isn't it? Thanks so such for inviting me."

The truth is that Suzy was pretty bad. Yet Rose, as a caring aunt, wanted to say nice things. Everything she said was true. A lot of work had gone into the play, and the play was very well-written. There were even some touching moments. But Rose never says that Suzy did a terrific job, that she's a great actress. In fact, her subtext clearly sent a message of: "It was nice, but don't quit your day job."

Now let's say Suzy has AD/HD, and perhaps she has difficulty reading subtext. She usually goes on the basis of the text, the words that are said. So afterward she tells her mom, "Aunt Rose loved the play! She said I touched her heart! Maybe I ought to become a professional actress like her!"

Well, that would be a mistake. And her mom would want to tell her so—in clear, honest words. Brutal honesty often turns subtext into text for those who missed the cues in a more gentle form.

It may seem that subtext is a whole different world. It's like the radio waves that are all around you, but you never pick them up if you don't have a radio. In the movie *The Matrix*, the Keanu Reeves character had to work very hard to discover that another world actually existed. It can be like that with conversational subtext. You may find it hard enough just to get through routine activities. Unfortunately, there's usually not much energy left to decipher this hidden language.

As with the other social skills covered in this book, subtext is something most people learn about growing up. It's no surprise that it's a child who breaks the news to the emperor about his "new clothes." Little children don't know much about reading between the lines—or speaking between the lines, for that matter. But by the time they're teenagers, they know.

Children learn social skills, like subtext-reading, from examples. As they watch and hear older people in conversation, paying attention to the details of pace, inflection, body language, etc., they learn to understand a full range of meaning. However, as you know, this is not always the case for those with AD/HD. It's tough to pay attention to those details, and so subtext can remain a mystery. Unless you work at learning and deciphering it, you probably won't just pick it up.

Unraveling the Subtext

If you were to read the script of a movie you've seen, you'd be amazed at how little it says. The lines themselves don't say a whole lot, but when the actors speak them, somehow they are filled with meaning.

"So you're going?"
"I think it's best."
"If you must."

As you read that text, it seems like a real yawner. But give those lines to a couple of great actors, and the text becomes emotionally wrenching. You know that he doesn't want to leave, and she wants him to stay, but neither one wants to admit how much they love each other. What they say is pretty

167

ordinary, but what they're not saying brings tears to your eyes.

How do actors make masterpieces out of ordinary lines? They search for the subtext. What is this character thinking and feeling? Why does he say these words? What do they want to happen? What do they expect? What are they trying to accomplish? All of these questions help the actors understand the subtext—the meaning between the lines.

Some acting teachers talk about the script as an iceberg. What you see is the tip, maybe ten percent of the entire iceberg. In the same way, the written, spoken lines are what you see and hear, but there's nine times that much under the surface. Sometimes beginning actors just play the tip of the iceberg. They say the lines, and they say them well, but they have no clue *why* they're saying those lines. As a result, the performance is "flat." There's little meaning there.

But good actors take the time to analyze the subtext, and then they reveal the whole iceberg. Their gestures, inflections, and expressions come from the total feelings of the character, not just the words that are said.

In life, people do the same sort of thing. Their words are just the tip of an iceberg of meaning. If you just hear the words, you're missing a lot of what's really going on. But you can learn to uncover the rest of that iceberg. People indirectly reveal what they really think and feel. Once you become aware that the subtext exists, you can begin to look for it.

The next step is to work on recognizing the clues of subtext. If we're talking about "reading between the lines," you have to learn a whole new alphabet. What does it mean when someone looks down or up, clears their throat, stammers, or raises an eyebrow? These can all be clues about the true meaning of the text.

You may need a tutor, a coach, someone to help you interpret the subtext until you become better able to see it. At work, for example, you may want to ask a well-liked colleague to help you understand what's really going on. After a meeting, together you can review what you think went on. "I heard the boss say such-and-such. Is that what he really meant, or did I miss something?"

Mary's company held a conference to rework its mission statement, and Mary was asked to give a pre-

sentation. She prepared diligently, creating worksheets with the current mission statement and suggestions for adjustments.

But once she began her presentation, she could tell from her boss's body language that something was wrong. He was fidgeting with papers, making scowling faces, and looking away. He didn't seem happy.

What's the problem? she wondered. She was doing exactly what he had asked her to do—lead the group in reworking the mission statement. But maybe she had misunderstood. Mary made suggestions about a few minor changes to the statement, a few wild stabs at a different approach. Maybe that would make the boss happy.

But no, he still looked upset. Finally Mary decided to take a risk. "Instead of reworking the statement," she said, "maybe we could start fresh and create our own."

Her boss's demeanor immediately changed. He began to smile, looking interested and happy. She had hit paydirt.

But afterward, Mary wondered what had happened there. She clearly remembered him saying, "Rework the mission statement." But obviously that wasn't actually the job he wanted her to do. He actually wanted her to lead the group in creating a new mission statement. If he wanted her to throw it out and start from scratch, why didn't he say so? She didn't know. Maybe he felt he had to show loyalty to the company founders who had created the original statement. Nonetheless, his words had led Mary in the wrong direction. She had to figure out the right direction from his subtext.

Many of my clients with AD/HD tell me that life would be much, much easier if everyone would just stop playing these games and be clear about what they really want. I agree, but it's not going to happen. So instead of sulking about the way the game is played, work on learning ways to figure out

170

how to play the game better.

Here are three basic assumptions that you need to know to stay out of trouble with the subtext:

Assumption #1

Never assume that what someone says is *exactly* what they really mean.

Assumption #2

Don't assume that what someone asks you to do is *exactly* what they want you to do.

Assumption #3

Don't assume that because someone agrees to do something that they *really* want to do it.

TIPS TO HELP YOU
BECOME A SUBTEXT DETECTIVE

If you watch MTV you may have seen "pop-up videos," which are bubbles that appear on the screen to help you know what's really going on. It would be great if bubbles like that would pop up in our social lives just as they do on television. In a way they do. They pop up in a variety of looks and actions that accompany people's words. But you still need to play detective and decipher these hidden meanings.

1. Look for clues in your environment to help you decipher the subtext. Just like the great detectives of our time, be mindful of alternative possibilities and be observant. Watch what others are doing.

2. Be on the lookout for body language, tone of voice, the look of someone's eyes, or their behavior to help you interpret what they say. There may be clues in the person's voice to help you discover the subtext. Pauses and sighs in speech can be revealing.

3. Look for matches between people's words and behaviors. If they say they're sad and they're crying, that looks like a match. But if they say they're happy and their body is tensing up, they may not really mean it.

4. Look at the choice of words the person uses. For example, there are several possible responses to the question, "Do you want to go to the movies tonight?"

I'd love to.	Probably means yes.
I could.	Probably means they'd rather not.
If you want to.	Probably not, but I want to be with you so I'll go.
Sure	Maybe yes, maybe no.
Maybe	Probably not.

5. Remember the old saying, "actions speak louder than words." If someone's words say one thing but their actions reveal another, it would be wise to consider that their actions might be revealing their true feelings. At the beginning of this book, I told of my son Jarryd's confusion when John said, "Maybe I can play," but never called. He needed to learn that the

action of not calling indicated that he really didn't want to play, despite the nice words.

6. Find a guide to help you with this hidden language. Compare your understanding of reality with their understanding of reality. If there is a discrepancy, you might want to try the other person's interpretation and see what happens, especially if you usually get it wrong.

7. Learn to interpret polite behavior. If you pop in to visit with someone and they are just getting ready to sit down and eat, they may say, "It's okay! Why don't you join us?" But they're probably just being polite. They really don't want to visit right now. However, if you decline and they really insist that you stay, and they tell you how much food they have and how much they really want to see you, and so on—then they probably do want you to stay. No wonder people make so many make social blunders! *Please stay* can really mean *I wish you would go; this is inconvenient.* Or it could mean, *please stay, I want to visit with you.*

8. Be alert to what others are doing. At work there may be places where you can sit and places where you're not supposed to sit—all depending on your social status. Or there may be preferred parking spaces— marked or unmarked. Maybe everyone "just knows" that the president parks in the space closest to the door. If you don't pick that up, you could be in trouble. So look around you for clues about proper behavior, proper seating, proper parking, etc.

173

9. Allow people their personal space. Each person has a buffer zone, an amount of space they need around them in order to feel comfortable. This boundary is not clearly marked or defined—you just need to have a sense of it. The trick is to find a distance that is close enough but not too close. Yet this distance varies in different cultures and with different types of relationships. In U.S. culture, the appropriate social distances are generally as follows:

    0 to 18 inches: **Intimate distance** such as love relationships.

    18 inches to 4 feet: **Personal distance** such as a friendly conversation.

    4 to 7 feet: **Social distance** such as formal business.

    12 to 25 feet: **Public distance** such as lectures.[2]

    In general, the closer you are in a relationship, the closer you can be physically with that person. In most casual conversations, you'd be safe with a distance of 3-4 feet.

    People will let you know when you're too close for their comfort. Not in words, but in subtext. They may back away, lean back, or just seem uncomfortable. When you read those signals, step back and give them the room they need.

10. Be careful with touch—hugging, hands on shoulders, etc. In our culture, touching is more limited than in many others. Generally, apart from a hand-

174

shake, we touch only those closest to us. But even with this basic rule, there are personal preferences. Some love to touch others and be touched, even with people they hardly know. Others dislike being touched at all, even by close friends. Once again, observe the subtext. If a person shrinks back from a touch, stop touching.

11. Respect people's privacy. If people go off by themselves, they probably want to be alone. Respect their personal moments. If you find yourself interrupting a private moment, excuse yourself and read the subtext. They may say, "That's okay, it's good to see you." but do they mean it? It would be polite to offer to leave. Then if they beg you to stay, you can stay.

This applies to phone calling as well as personal visits. It's always nice to ask, "Do you have a minute to talk?" before starting a lengthy conversation. Try to avoid people's dinnertime or their best working time. Try not to call work colleagues on the weekend, unless you know they'd want you to. And be careful about calling (or visiting) late at night or early in the morning. If you must contact someone at an inopportune time, keep it short and to the point. Be sure to read the subtext, too. If there's any hint of irritation about calling or visiting at a bad time, apologize and set up a better time to talk.

Context

A socially competent individual is able to choose the appropriate social skill for a specific situation.[3] While reading the subtext is being aware of *what people mean*, reading the context is being aware of *where you are*. Different situations have different expectations. Unfortunately, these are not always clearly stated, so you need to observe what others are doing and "read" the expected behavior. Your actions and responses need to be appropriate to your situation.

Louis had worked hard on learning appropriate social skills and yet there was still another obstacle to overcome. "For the longest time," he told me, "whenever I would see someone, I would offer them a 'good morning.' The problem was, I wouldn't bother to register whether or not it was indeed morning, or noon, or night. It was always just 'good morning.' Nowadays, I know better, and I make sure of the time before I open my mouth."

To be sure, there are worse problems than saying, "Good morning," all the time. But Louis realized that this quirk set him apart as a guy who didn't know what was going on, and that was an identity he didn't want to have. Develop your awareness of what's appropriate in different contexts, so you look like you *do* know what's going on. Louis' behavior made him stand out like a sore thumb.

Appearance

Different situations call for different attire. It would look odd indeed if you wore a business suit to play softball. And you wouldn't want to wear your softball jersey to work.

Some businesses have dress codes, but many just have unwritten expectations. A suit and tie is pretty standard for men in the business world, but women have various options (suits, slacks, dresses). More and more people are working from home. That may ease the dress standards a bit for business meetings, but don't assume you can get away with jeans if you're lunching with a client or supplier.

Jan couldn't understand why she kept getting fired. She was a good secretary, typing 70 words per minute, with a lively personality. "I just don't get it," she complained loudly to her friend Marge on the phone one afternoon. "My boss gave me my review today and he said I was 'on probation.' Can you believe that? He said I should dress more conservatively—longer skirts, I guess. Something about the image of

177

the office, he said. Well, I don't have any longer skirts, I told him, and I think the image of the office could use a little lightening up. He didn't like that at all."

Sure, Jan was just being herself—her boisterous, raucous, short-skirted self. But if she really wanted to succeed at this job, she had to learn to play by the rules. And that meant accepting feedback from the boss and dressing appropriately for the office.

In general, everyone is dressing more casually. Not too long ago, everyone dressed up a bit to go out to eat, to the theater, or to church. Nowadays, some do, some don't. It often depends on *which* restaurant, theater, or church you're attending. At the places you want to go, look around and see what others are wearing. When in doubt, dress up more than down. It's better to look nice in a casual situation than to look sloppy in a formal situation.

QUICK TIP

Ask. When you're not sure what to wear, check with someone whose opinion you respect—someone with good social awareness. Ask them to help you uncover the hidden expectations. "I know we are having a company picnic on saturday. What are we supposed to wear?"

Behavior

There are certain things you can do that would only be understood in context. If you were seen driving around town dressed as a WWF wrestler, that would seem odd. Unless of course it was Halloween, in which case you'd look great. Dressing oddly is an expected behavior for Halloween.

You'd be considered incredibly rude if you were yelling at someone—unless of course you were at an ice hockey game in Philadelphia. In that context, being quiet would be the odd behavior.

You need to be aware of the context and adjust your behavior accordingly.

Language

Language also needs to vary based on the context. While you may talk very casually with a colleague in the hall, you may need to use much more formal language once you enter a meeting. Professions also have their own accepted vocabularies for formal meetings and presentations.

If you use profanities or obscenities, be sure to curtail it when you're with those who would be offended by it.

One friend told me of an insurance salesman who made a pitch salted with obscene words—possibly because he thought this would "bond" him with my friend, who was also male. It didn't work. My friend was turned off by the offensive language and refused to buy the policy.

But proper language can also be inappropriate in less formal situations. If you use only business terms with someone you're romantically interested in, the relationship will probably not go too far.

These are just some examples of different situations, requiring different skills. The important thing is to be aware of your setting and be observant of the special requirements of the different settings. And when in doubt—ASK!

JUST THE FACTS

- The **subtext** refers to the meaning behind what is actually being said or done.

- People don't always say what they mean because they may be afraid to hurt our feelings, or they may be afraid of the consequences of saying what they really mean

- Never assume that what someone says is *exactly* what they really mean.

- Don't assume that what someone asks you to do is *exactly* what they want you to do.

- Don't assume that because someone agrees to do something that they *really* want to do it.

- Discover the subtext by: (1) asking questions for clarification and (2) watching what others are doing.

- Different situations have different expectations— **context.**

- Be sure your appearance, behavior, and language are appropriate for the context.

NOTES

1. Lavoie, R. (1994). *Learning disabilities and social skills: last one picked...first one picked on.* Washington, D.C.: WETA-TV.
2. Taylor, S., Peplau, L., & Sears, D. (1997). *Social psychology.* Upper Saddle River, New Jersey: Prentice Hall. p. 418.
3. Elksnin, L., & Elksnin, N. (1995). *Assessment and instruction of social skills.* San Diego: Singular Publishing Group, Inc. p. 12.

Chapter 10

On the See-Saw
Interpersonal
Relationship Skills

BARBARA AND BETTY both have AD/HD. Barbara always seems to be the life of the party. Barbara seems to have a million friends. She is always going out and her phone is always ringing. Or at least so it seems to Betty, who finds it difficult to make friends and even more difficult to keep them. Although both struggle with AD/HD, they are in very different places in their social worlds.

Many people have been trying to figure out what makes one person popular and another not. If you've been pondering this question, you're not alone. In fact, for quite a while now social psychologists and researchers have been trying to discover why we tend to like one person more than another. What are the general characteristics of those who are generally liked versus those who are generally not liked? So far they have found that at the top of the likability list are six traits related to trust: trustworthiness, sincerity, honesty, loyalty, truthfulness, and dependability. Trust seems to be very

183

important in being liked. The traits rated lowest included dishonesty and phoniness. Let's take a look at a more complete list of these traits and where they stack up in terms of likability.

Likability of Personality Traits [1]

Highly Likable	Highly Unlikable
Sincere	Ill-mannered
Honest	Unfriendly
Understanding	Hostile
Loyal	Loud-mouthed
Truthful	Selfish
Trustworthy	Narrow-minded
Intelligent	Rude
Dependable	Conceited
Thoughtful	Greedy
Considerate	Insincere
Reliable	Unkind
Warm	Untrustworthy
Kind	Malicious
Friendly	Obnoxious
Happy	Untruthful
Unselfish	Dishonest
Humorous	Cruel
Responsible	Mean
Cheerful	Phony
Trustful	Lying

Where do you see yourself? To be better liked, you'd want to demonstrate traits on the highly likeable side of the list as much as possible. It's also a good idea to avoid or at least limit the characteristics on the highly unlikeable side of the list.

According to **social exchange theory**, our liking for another person is based on our assessment of the costs and benefits the person provides us.[2] We like people when we perceive our interactions with them to be profitable—that is, the benefits we get from the relationship outweigh the costs. The likability list confirms this. When people demonstrate the well-liked traits on the left, they benefit the people around them. On the other hand, the unlikeable traits are hurtful and costly to the surrounding people.

Most of us have mixtures of these traits, and our level of likability depends on a weighing of the two sides. Therefore, people may like Stan because he's smart, funny, and a good athlete; these good qualities outweigh his annoying tendency to be late. Often on an unconscious level, people become "social accountants." They try to arrange their interpersonal relationships to get the most benefits and minimize their costs.

To receive benefits, however, we must also provide them to others. Remember the see-saw image from an earlier chapter. Relationships involve give and take, and it's important to keep up your end of the giving. According to social psychologists, there are several basic kinds of *benefits* to give and to get—including money, goods, services, love, status, and information.

Costs are the negative consequences that occur in a relationship. A relationship might be viewed as costly, for example, if it requires a great deal of our time and energy, because it creates conflict or because others disapprove of it. So even when you're not aware of it, the process of interaction creates benefits and costs for the people involved.

People are most content when they perceive their social relationships to be fair. People don't like to feel exploited by others, nor do people generally like to take advantage of others. People generally try to seek balance in relationships.

185

Again we have that see-saw image of give and take.

Social exchange theory assumes that, on some level, people keep track of the benefits and costs of a relationship. We don't usually make lists of the good and bad things about a relationship, but we're still aware of the costs and benefits. Most people have a general sense of the overall quality of their relationships. When people say, "I'm really getting a lot out of this relationship," or "I don't think our relationship is worth it anymore," those are social cost-benefit analyses.

High Maintenance Relationships

Those with AD/HD are often considered to be "high mainte-nance." It can be fun and stimulating to be with someone who is hyperactive and impulsive, but it can also be exhaust-ing. It's difficult for those without AD/HD to maintain the enthusiasm and energy they need to keep up with the rapidly changing ideas and impulses of people with AD/HD.

It's also a challenge to be with someone who has AD/HD *without* hyperactivity. It may require less physical effort, but it takes great emotional energy to help such people gather, track, and share their ideas. After years of rejection, some of you have learned to be quiet. To protect yourself, you may have shut down. It takes nurturing, encouragement, and sen-sitivity on the part of others to help to draw you out.

Many people enter social relationships to get their own needs met, not to meet the other person's needs. There's an attentive stretch required to focus on someone else's needs. It's a lot easier to concentrate on your own. But, long-lasting social relationships are all about give and take. If you put any stock in the social exchange theory, you'll need to make every effort to keep your relationships in balance.

Behaviors that Build Relationships

What can you do to be a better friend? How can you make a relationship with you more of a positive experience for others?

Sharing/Helping. Look outside of yourself and reach out to help others. This will build your self-esteem as well as your social stature. People like to be associated with people they consider helpful. So helping others is good for you and good for others.

Smiles/Laughter. Try to have a positive outlook on life. Saying positive things about people, things, and events should increase your popularity. People tend to be attracted to those who smile, laugh, and are just plain fun to be around; they get tired of hanging around those who always seem angry or upset.

Compromise/Negotiation. At some point in any relationship, you will need to resolve differences. For effective negotiation, you need to learn to compromise. Approach the problem in an open, positive manner. Hostility rarely gets you the result you desire. If you have a "win at any cost" attitude, others will not feel valued. You might get your way, but you could easily lose a friend. Try to create a win-win situation where everyone comes out ahead.

Advocating/Empathizing. Sometimes people with AD/HD get ignored. As a result, they're often isolated from others. To keep this from happening, you need to learn to *advocate* for yourself—that is, stand up for yourself, speak up about your own needs—not in a belligerent way, but assertively. This may involve being honest about your struggles with AD/HD and asking for some help.

But it can't be all about you. Learn to "advocate" for others, too. Pay attention to the needs of others. Think about how they must be feeling, too. If you can balance your self-

187

advocating with empathy for others, people will consider you a valuable friend.

Styles of Conflict Management

Conflict occurs in all sorts of relationships and people have different styles of addressing it. *How* you deal with interpersonal problems has a major effect on how well you maintain friendships. At a recent seminar, several people *without* AD/HD told me how their family members *with* AD/HD dealt with disagreements.

"I've taught my 21-year-old college student son with ADD to learn to advocate for himself," said one woman, "but I don't think that he has it quite right. So he got a D on his biology test instead of the expected B. Just like his mother taught him, he tried to advocate. He goes up to the teacher and instead of saying, 'Can I talk about this with you?' he said, 'You made a —— mistake.' I call his style 'advocating to alienate.' I don't think he understands that 'advocate' doesn't mean to pound on the other person."

Another woman told me the following story.

"My 18-year-old son has ADD. What gets him into trouble is seeing things so black-and-white that he can't give anyone else's opinion the benefit of the doubt. My husband, who also has ADD, is like that too. Even if my husband makes a suggestion to me, I know that it's not really just a suggestion. It's his way or no way.

Both of them are like that and they absolutely railroad people. They're both nice people, but they don't realize how

188

*that destroys relationships—not valuing other people's opin-
ions or at least even pretending to. . . . My son is in high
school and it's a particular problem. If he has a different
opinion than somebody else, he doesn't just politely accept
theirs. He says, 'That's stupid,' and the next thing you know,
he can't figure out why he is left out of things.*

People have different styles in addressing conflict. I've
identified five types of conflict management styles according to the characteristics of certain animals. Where do you
fit in?

1. **The Fox.** Some approach conflict as a purely logical process, unaware of the feelings involved—their
   own or others'.

2. **The Turtle.** Some try to avoid all conflict. They
   withdraw from conflict situations.

3. **The Bull.** When faced with conflict, they over-
   power others. Often inconsiderate of others, they
   only see things from their own point of view. It's
   "my way or the highway."

4. **The Puppy Dog.** They always try to smooth over
   differences, often putting others first. They're nice
   people, but they're generally not effective in getting their own needs met.

5. **The Wise Owl.** Aware of their own needs and feelings as well as the needs and feelings of others,
   they are willing to compromise and look for creative ways to get everyone's needs met.

TIPS TO HELP
WITH CONFLICT RESOLUTION

1. Make sure you clearly understand the different sides of the conflict.

2. Respect yourself and others.

3. Discuss the various options and their probable outcomes.

4. Think "outside the box," looking for ideas that have not yet been considered.

5. Determine the relative importance to both parties. Some things are just more important to a person than other things.

6. Choose the best alternative, keeping in mind the value of relationships as well as the problem at hand.

Anger Management

Let's face it, sometimes you get mad. And you're not alone. Everybody gets mad sometimes. Anger is a natural response to a perceived injustice. As you see it, something just isn't right or fair, and you're upset about it. Sometimes anger is the result of not getting what we want.

People do different things with their anger. Some may be afraid to feel angry or to express anger. Some may not even realize they're angry; they suppress their anger and act as if it's not there. Others explode at the slightest provocation and rage like a thunderstorm. They may yell and even throw and break things. There are also people in between.

Lots of people *without* AD/HD get angry, so obviously the anger problem isn't limited to those with AD/HD. But AD/HD makes life more challenging and more frustrating sometimes. And this frustration may often boil over into anger. In addition, the impulsive nature of AD/HD can make it difficult to control angry outbursts at times.

Managing Your Anger

One problem with anger is that feelings can overwhelm facts; passion floods your mind and makes you do irrational things. When you begin to feel angry, it's crucial to keep your wits about you. In fact, you can learn to use your wit to win the battle with anger. Use the acronym: WIT WON, to help you remember the following tip:

Wait
I Messages
Tell your story

Wish Statements
Other side
Negotiate

Wait. Select the best time and place to express your anger. It's hard to resolve a dispute properly when either person is tired, busy, or frustrated. It's better to schedule a future time and place to talk about your concern, rather than insist on doing it *now*.

191

Stephanie is just coming in the door from work, exhausted from her busy day. Her husband greets her with, "I'm mad! I don't have the shirt I need for that meeting tonight and you promised you'd wash one for me!"

Freeze frame. What happens next? A major argument? Possibly. Stephanie could lash back with, "Why do I have to do everything around here? Can't you even get dressed yourself? And what about that leaky faucet you promised to fix three weeks ago?"

Oh, there's plenty of ammunition for an all-out fight. But this isn't the time. Stephanie is worn out from work, and her husband is uptight about his meeting. In that situation, both would say hurtful things. Although the shirt matter might need quick attention, allowing Stephanie a few minutes to relax and unwind would greatly improve the situation.

"When's your meeting, hon?" she might ask. "Seven-thirty? Well, give me 10 minutes to crash and then I'll take care of your shirt, okay?" Her wit wins out, and her soft answer calms her husband's anger.

But there's one more scene that needs to take place in this drama. Later that night, after his meeting, after Stephanie has taken a long, relaxing bath, they need to talk about this again.

"Honey," she needs to say, "I know you were upset about the shirt and anxious about your meeting, but I really felt overwhelmed when I walked through the door. I forgot about the shirt, and I'm sorry. But we both make mistakes like that. Give me a chance to breathe first, and then we can work things out."

Waiting for the right time can help set the stage for resolution.

QUICK TIP

While you're waiting for a good time to talk, you may find it helpful to engage in some type of physical activity as an outlet for your anger. Pillow-punching, running, walking, making bread—find the physical outlet that works best for you. Emotional outlets such as letter-writing can also help to manage your anger. Writing your thoughts and feelings can also help you to organize what you would like to say.

"I" Messages. When you state your concern, use "I" messages rather than "you" messages. An "I" message conveys your concern based on what *you* are feeling or sensing. The "you" message blames the other person. Such "acc-you-sations" only tend to make situations worse.

You didn't call me when you said you would. (You message)

I was worried when I didn't hear from you. (I message)

"I" statements make your message less threatening than "you" messages. They are not as likely to put others in an uncomfortable, defensive position. "I" messages set the stage for communication and healing in relationships.

Tell Your Story. Give a few highlights, and only a few highlights, to help others understand your experience or concerns. Keep focused on the issue. Do not overwhelm others with a number of other issues or too many details. Sometimes AD/HD makes it difficult to stay focused. If you bring in a lot of tangential thoughts, it will be difficult for others to follow you.

QUICK TIP

You may find it helpful to write some notes on an index card to help you stay on track.

WISH Statement. After you've had the opportunity to express your feelings, let others know what you would like them *to do.* It is best to state this as a wish, rather than a demand.

Next time you must call me. (Demand statement)

When this comes up in the future, I wish that you would call me so I won't worry. (Wish statement)

Can you see the difference in the wording? Demands can be very stressful on relationships. And often they don't work. On the other hand, wishes set the stage for healing.

Other Side. No story has only one side. Allow others to tell their story and share their concerns—and really listen. Don't interrupt. Use reflective listening—the echo approach—to let the person know you're listening. Try to understand the story from their perspective rather than just being caught up in your anger.

194

Negotiation. Once both of you have had the opportunity to express your feelings, tell your story, hear the story of the other person, and once you've had the opportunity to state your wish, you are ready to wrap this up. Creatively look for a win-win resolution for your discussion. Remember, the purpose of working on anger management is to help you keep and develop deeper relationships. Sometimes you may need to concede a particular issue, but if you maintain the relationship that you wanted, you still win. Winning is often in the eye of the beholder.

With regard to conflict in a romantic relationship, Jonathan Halverstadt, author of *A.D.D. and Romance*, felt that the following statement is so important it should be tattooed on your brain or at least written on your hand: "Most conflicts in a romantic relationship are not about the conflict—they are about significance." [3]

If people don't feel valued in a relationship, they will argue about the slightest thing. In addition, they will find it difficult to resolve their differences. On the other hand, if people feel valued and cared for, compromise and negotiations are usually easily handled.

Valuing people and letting them know that you value them is a key to successful negotiation.

Get Help

If you continue to have anger management difficulties, consider seeking professional help. Many difficulties with anger can be helped through counseling. At times the anger may just be the tip of the iceberg, with a number of additional emotional issues buried beneath. Counseling is a safe and productive setting to explore these issues and discover alternative solutions.

TIPS FOR HELPING SOMEONE ELSE MANAGE THEIR ANGER

1. **Stabilize.** Constructive dialogue is very difficulty until the angry person is calm. This is best done by YOU remaining calm. Avoid escalating your behavior to match their behavior. Maintain an even tone of voice and low-key body language. It will eventually help to calm down the angry person as they begin to match your behavior.

2. **Go with the flow.** Use "emotional judo." Flow *with* the anger, rather then trying to fight against it. This allows the angry person to vent without escalating the situation. They eventually should run out of steam and be in a better position to talk. If you push against the anger, the anger is fed and will grow.

3. **Try to understand the anger.** Everyone has reasons for what they do and what they feel. By seeking to understand their world, you can often understand what angers them.

4. **Encourage them to find a physical outlet for their anger.** Any physical exercise or task can be extremely helpful in de-escalating anger.

5. **Get out.** If the person is so angry that you fear physical or emotional harm, immediately leave the situation. You can approach the person at a different time when it's safer.

Becoming Assertive

Assertive behavior is the ability to stand up for yourself and exercise your rights in a comfortable manner without denying or infringing upon the rights of others. Acting in an assertive manner requires that you (1) know what you need or want and (2) are able to express those needs in an effective and appropriate way.

Assertiveness is an important interpersonal skill. You don't want to be a pushover and yet you don't want to appear too aggressive. If you're too passive, you may feel hurt, anxious, or self-demeaning. Usually it's the social fear of being disliked or rejected that stops people from acting assertively. Although a passive person may avoid an unpleasant situation for the moment, often frustration will build as personal needs go unmet. At times this can even lead to depression or anxiety.

On the other hand, if you come on too strong and react out of anger you may hurt or offend others. Aggressive behavior leads to disrupted communication and broken interpersonal relationships.

The word "assert" means to state or affirm positively, assuredly, plainly, or strongly. In therapeutic terms an assertive person demonstrates the following four characteristics:

1. *Assertive people feel free to reveal themselves.* Through words and actions they say, "This is what I think, this is what I feel—this is me."

2. *An assertive person can communicate* with people in an open, direct, honest, and appropriate manner that does not offend others.

197

3. *They have an assertive orientation to life.* Assertive people go after what they want, in contrast to the passive person, who usually waits for things to happen.

4. *An assertive person behaves in a manner that is respectful* to both themselves and others.

If you don't tell people how you feel and what you think, you deny them the opportunity to change. And if you steamroll over people, you won't have relationships.

Effective assertive behavior does not always get you what you want, but it does help you feel good about yourself without alienating others. Others usually respect the assertive individual.

If you're having difficulty in this area, you could seek help through an assertiveness training course, additional readings in this area, or professional coaching or counseling. Most people can learn to find the balance once they understand the problem.

EXERCISES

Assertiveness Skills

Observation

1. Watch people interacting. Find people acting in a passive, assertive, and aggressive manner.
2. Watch the reactions of those they are talking with. What do their faces and body language tell you?
3. What happens as a result of their behavior?
4. Can you pick up any ideas from the assertive person?

Evaluation

1. Identify a recent situation where you feel that you missed the assertive mark.
2. Were you too passive or too aggressive?
3. Given the time to think about the situation, how could you have handled the situation in a more assertive manner?
4. Shut your eyes and visualize yourself acting differently. Imagine yourself in the same situation, but this time imagine yourself acting in an assertive manner.

Action

1. Try to identify an upcoming opportunity to act in an assertive manner.
2. Think about how you would like to behave.
3. Shut your eyes and visualize yourself acting in an assertive manner.
4. Practice this several times before you have the opportunity to use your assertive skills.
5. Good luck!!!

JUST THE FACTS

- There are certain characteristics of people who are generally liked and those who are generally not liked. Review the list at the beginning of this chapter.

- At the top of the likability list are traits related to trust: trustworthiness, sincerity, honesty, loyalty, truthfulness, and dependability. The traits rated lowest include dishonesty and phoniness. People tend to be attracted to people who smile, laugh, and are fun to be around.

- According to **social exchange theory** our liking for another person is based on our assessment of the costs and benefits of the relationship.

- Relationships create benefits and costs for the people involved. Those with AD/HD are often considered to be "high maintenance." It's important to balance out relationships.

- How you deal with interpersonal problems has a major effect on how well you maintain friendships. There are different styles of conflict resolution. The wisest people are willing to compromise and look for creative ways to get everyone's needs met.

- When dealing with anger, learn to use your *wit to win*.

Wait for a good time to discuss issues.

I messages say how *you* feel rather than blaming the *other person*.

Tell your story. Stay focused on the issue at hand. Rein in tangential thoughts.

Wish statements. State your desire as a wish, rather than a demand.

Other side. Listen to the other side of the story.

Negotiate. Look for a win-win situation.

- Find the physical outlet that seems to work best for you and then use it when you become angry.

- You don't want to be a pushover, and yet you don't want to appear too aggressive. Assertiveness is the middle you'll want to strive for.

NOTES

1. Anderson, N.H. (1968). Likeableness ratings of 555 personality-trait words. *Journal of Social Psychology, 9,* 272-279. Cited in S. Taylor, L. Peplau and D. Sears, *Social psychology* (1997). *(9th ed.),* Upper Saddle River, New Jersey: Prentice Hall. p. 235.

2. Taylor, S., Peplau, l., & Sears, D. (1997). *Social psychology (9th ed.).* Upper Saddle River, New Jersey: Prentice Hall. p. 235.

3. Halverstadt, J. (1998). *A.D.D. and romance: Finding fulfillment in love, sex, & relationships.* Dallas: Taylor Publishing Co. p. 105.

Part Four

Improving Social Skills

Chapter 11

How am I Doing?:
Inventory of Strengths & Growth Areas

HAVE YOU EVER been lost in a mall? You don't know where to go until you know where you are. Usually you walk over to the big map with the bright-colored squares and try to orient yourself. *Now there's Sears, there's B. Dalton, and I just passed the Old Navy.* There's always a sigh of relief when you can find that little mark that says, "You are here." Once you discover where you are, it is easier to know where to go.

205

The same is true for life in general—especially life with AD/HD. Goals are best set once you understand where you are. As you work toward your goals, you need to keep figuring out where you are, how you're doing, and how you're progressing. Are you getting where you need to be?

This book should be giving you ideas of social skills you'd like to improve or develop. But, in order to get the big picture, it would help to know your current social skills. Does your social life need some minor tinkering or a major overhaul? By getting an assessment of the social skills you have now, you can paste a big "You are here!" sticker on the map of your social life.

Detecting Your Sources

How do you figure out what social skills you have? Well, you could analyze it by yourself, but you may not have the most accurate image. You certainly know *some* aspects of your social situation, but everyone has blind spots about their own behavior. Others may have some of the missing pieces to the puzzle.

We can understand this "puzzle" a bit better with a model taken from group therapy called the Johari Window. [1]

Johari Window

1. What you and others know about you.	3. What you do not know about yourself but others do.
2. What you know about yourself but others do not.	4. What you and others do not know about you.

206

Box 1—What you and others know about you. This refers to all the things that are known to you and visible to others. We might call this "common knowledge." For example, you are tall, you have a deep voice.

Box 2—What you know about yourself but others do not. This refers to those private thoughts and feelings that you have, but don't share with others. These are your secrets. For example, you may be very lonely, but you hide it with smiles and laughter, so others don't know.

Box 3—What you do not know about yourself but others do. This is your blind side. For example, you might always interrupt people when they're talking, and in your excitement to share your ideas you may never have realized this. It's obvious to others, but not to you.

This is the most important box to add to your picture in trying to assess your social skills. Other people have information about you, but they won't tell you unless you ask. Maybe they're being polite, or they think you don't want to hear it, but in any case they have chosen not to share these observations with you. Others close to you probably know what social skills you most need to work on. They can see your blind side.

Box 4—What you and others do not know about you. In psychology we know that there is always more. Don't worry about this box for now. If it's important, it will become visible to you or those close to you when the time is right.

Self Report

The first part of this discovery process is for you to look *inward* and assess where you feel you are with regard to social skills. I have included a checklist (*Novotni Social Skills Checklist*) for you to complete about how you view your strengths well as areas that need work. It will be most helpful to you if you accurately and honestly represent yourself on the checklist. The checklist is only for your use. You will not be graded on this! For privacy, there is a copy of this checklist in the Appendix which you can copy to keep apart from the book.

Reports from Others

The second part of the process is to look *outward* and discover what others think about your social skills. Get feedback from the people closest to you. Start with two people you trust, perhaps one family member and one friend from your job or from the neighborhood. What do they see as your strengths and areas you need to grow in?

I have also included checklists for others to complete. They can be found in the Appendix. Assure them that you want their honest feedback. Often people are afraid to be completely truthful about their perceptions, because they don't want to hurt your feelings.

So how do you get others to tell you their truthful opinions about you? You need to create an atmosphere in which the other person feels safe in offering honest feedback. Remember, that they may be seeing a part of you that you're not aware of so be open to hearing them, especially if several people tell you the same things.

Novotni Social Skills Checklist—Self Report

Traits

How many of the following traits of highly likeable people are descriptive of you? Circle all that apply. Put a check by the ones you would like to work on:

sincere	honest	understanding	loyal
truthful	trustworthy	intelligent	warm
thoughtful	considerate	reliable	kind
responsible	friendly	unselfish	trustful
humorous	cheerful	dependable	

Use the following checklist to identify strengths as well as areas to work on.

NOT A PROBLEM	NEEDS IMPROVEMENT	
		BASIC MANNERS: The ability to do the following in your social interactions with others.
_____	_____	• Use mannerly words like please, thank you, and you're welcome
_____	_____	• Express appreciation
_____	_____	• Receive compliments without discounting
_____	_____	• Give compliments regularly to others
_____	_____	• Apologize
_____	_____	• Accept the apology of others
_____	_____	• Introduce yourself
_____	_____	• Introduce others
_____	_____	• Use appropriate greetings
_____	_____	• Use appropriate ending comments
_____	_____	• Phone manners
_____	_____	• Mealtime behaviors (follow lead of host/hostess, chew with mouth closed, don't talk when mouth full, ask to have items passed, use napkins, elbows off the table, ask to be excused)
_____	_____	• Making others feel comfortable in your home—hosting
_____	_____	• Offer to help others

Note: From Michele Novotni, *What Does Everybody Else Know That I Don't?* Copyright 1999 by Specialty Press, Inc. This form may be reproduced for personal use.

NOT A PROBLEM	NEEDS IMPROVEMENT	
		II. VERBAL COMMUNICATION SKILLS:
		In conversation with others the ability to:
_____	_____	• Join a conversation without disruption
_____	_____	• Check—repeat what you heard and ask if you heard it right
_____	_____	• Identify and reflect *content* of conversation—tracking
_____	_____	• Identify and reflect *feelings* of others
_____	_____	• Ability to reflect content + feelings in conversations
_____	_____	• Use minimal encouragers to let others know you are following the conversation
_____	_____	• Use open questions to keep conversations going
_____	_____	• Ask for help when needed or desired

III. NONVERBAL COMMUNICATION SKILLS: Looking attentive when listening. When talking with others do you:

_____	_____	• Keep an open posture
_____	_____	• Face the person
_____	_____	• Lean forward
_____	_____	• Maintain appropriate eye contact
_____	_____	• Look relaxed

IV. COMMUNICATION ROADBLOCKS

_____	_____	• Miss pieces of information—"blinks"
_____	_____	• Use closed or naked questions
_____	_____	• Voice too loud or too soft
_____	_____	• Speak too quickly
_____	_____	• Interrupt others
_____	_____	• Too quiet—rarely speaking in conversations
_____	_____	• Talk excessively
_____	_____	• Order or boss others
_____	_____	• Critical—judge or evaluate others
_____	_____	• Minimize or not be considerate

V. ORGANIZATIONAL SKILLS—TRUSTWORTHY

_____	_____	• Difficulty with deadlines
_____	_____	• Difficulty being on time for meetings and appointments

210

NOT A PROBLEM   **NEEDS IMPROVEMENT**

———————   ———————   • Dificulty remembering special occasions

———————   ———————   • Too organized, rigid
———————   ———————   • Difficulty managing money, bills, bank accounts, etc.
———————   ———————   • Difficulty organizing your stuff
———————   ———————   • Do what you agree to do
———————   ———————   • Finish projects

VI. SELF CONTROL

———————   ———————   • Take turns/wait
———————   ———————   • Ability to handle inappropriate behavior of others
———————   ———————   • Effectively manage conflict, negotiate and compromise
———————   ———————   • Effectively manage anger
———————   ———————   • Refrain from aggressive behavior
———————   ———————   • Assertiveness
———————   ———————   • Impulsive spending
———————   ———————   • Impulsive decision-making
———————   ———————   • Filter thoughts avoiding impulsive words—blurting things that hurt people
———————   ———————   • Inappropriate touch of others
———————   ———————   • Difficulty relaxing
———————   ———————   • Excessive physical activity (trouble staying seated, fidget, feeling restless)

VII. KNOWLEDGE

———————   ———————   • Understand *attribution theory*'s role in social relationships
———————   ———————   • Understand the importance of *social exchange theory*—give and take in relationships
———————   ———————   • Understand the subtle cues that you give others with your body language
———————   ———————   • Ability to pick up the *subtext*—socially perceptive
———————   ———————   • Understand *context*

VIII. RELATIONSHIPS

———————   ———————   • Sensitive to the needs of others
———————   ———————   • Patient
———————   ———————   • Creative

211

NOT A PROBLEM	NEEDS IMPROVEMENT	
_____	_____	• Fun to be with
_____	_____	• Flexible—able to go with the flow
_____	_____	• Respect boundary of others
_____	_____	• Treat others with respect
_____	_____	• Tolerance to differences of others
_____	_____	• Initiate invitations to others
_____	_____	• Difficulty with intimacy
_____	_____	• Have at least three close friends

IX. SELF CARE

_____	_____	• Ability to nurture yourself
_____	_____	• Appearance—clean, neat, and appropriate for situations
_____	_____	• Ability to identify and express your feelings
_____	_____	• Self-esteem
_____	_____	• Participate in support groups
_____	_____	• Sense of humor
_____	_____	• Positive outlook—hope

What is the most important area for you to work on to improve your social relationships?

_____ Basic Manners

_____ Verbal Communication Skills

_____ Nonverbal Communication Skills

_____ Communication Roadblocks

_____ Organizational Skills

_____ Self Control

_____ Knowledge

_____ Relationships

_____ Self Care

TIPS FOR ASKING FOR FEEDBACK

Are you ready for this? It can be tough to hear the truth about yourself from others. You'll need thick skin, and a willingness and openness to receive criticism. If you're not ready, you might get angry or defensive and say things that could damage a good relationship. But if you really want to get the big picture of your social skills, get ready to hear about some areas that need a little work.

1. **Ask for their opinion in an open and nondefensive manner.** For example, *"John, I am working on making improvements in my social skills. For me to do this, it would be real helpful to know how others see me. Can I ask you for your honest feedback? It would really help me."*

2. Once the person has taken the risk to answer the questionnaire, **DO NOT argue with them about their opinion.** If you strongly disagree, remember that you do not have to act on their feedback. That is merely their perspective at this time and it was very nice of them to share this information with you.

3. **Thank them for their feedback and support.** For example, *"Thanks, John, for taking your time to fill this out, and most of all for your honesty. I will look into what you have told me. Thanks again."*

4. Now that you're aware of their perspective, **test out** the validity of their comments as you interact socially. Were they right about you or not?

I once had a client who was a medical student—obviously very intelligent, but desperately struggling with social difficulties. He had many acquaintances, but no friends. Though he tried to figure out what was wrong, he wasn't making any progress. In counseling, I gave him questionnaires to have his family members and acquaintances complete to help us both understand his difficulties better.

He went home excited and faxed copies of a questionnaire to 23 family members and acquaintances. He got most of them back. In fact, they were so helpful to him that he canceled his counseling sessions. He now understood what was causing his social difficulties, thanks to the information given to him.

Others had never told him this information, or perhaps they had gently tried but he wasn't listening. Once he asked, however, they were more than willing to try to help him.

People you know can be a gold mine of information for you, if you just ask.

Setting Goals: Where do you want to go?

There's a potato chip commercial that says, "Bet you can't eat just one!" Because the potato chips taste good, it's difficult to stop eating them. Well, the same can be true in the area of goal setting. Sometimes it's extremely difficult to stop at just one goal. However, it's important to choose only one growth area at a time.

I know you may be getting excited about improving all these skills. In the excitement, you may have a desire to work on 10 things at once. But it's better in the long run to pick one goal and work on this goal until you have been successful. Then move on to your next goal. By working on one goal at a time, you'll have a sense of progress, and you'll feel better about yourself in the process.

One goal at a time will keep you working. You may have a tendency to fill your mind with millions of goals. But you need to let go of some of these goals to work more effectively. Henry David Thoreau said it best, "Simplify. Simplify. Simplify."

Especially with AD/HD, a single focus is helpful. It's an AD/HD trait to flit from thing to thing. But if you don't stay focused on one, you may never master any. If you prioritize your goals and choose one enjoyable, reachable goal, you'll be more likely to succeed.

Review your checklist and the checklists of others. Make a list of all the goals you would like to work on. For now, select just one goal. Yes, just one! If you master that one, you can repeat this process until your social skills have improved to the level you desire. Here are some tips to help you choose your goal.

TIPS TO SELECT YOUR GOAL

- **Quick Success**. Choose a goal which you feel you can accomplish fast. This quick success can help feed the cycle of success. Don't tackle your toughest goals first. Practice first on some of the easier goals to help you increase your self-confidence and build momentum.

- **Motivation**. What is it that *you* really want to work on? Choose to work only on goals that you have a personal investment in. It's difficult to work on changes unless you are really motivated.

215

- **Prioritize goals**. One of the exciting features of AD/HD is the enthusiasm and excitement that often accompany it. Ideas swirl and energy flows. Sometimes, however, everything looks equally important or appealing. If you are having a difficult time understanding what is truly most important, ask someone else to help you keep your priorities in line.

- **Reduce expectations**. Happiness is the result of accomplishing what you want to do. So if you set your expectations too high and you fail, you won't be pleased—even though you accomplished quite a bit. But if you set your expectations lower and you reach your goal, you'll be happy. Perspective is important.

- **Small steps**. Even the largest, most overwhelming changes are made one step at a time. There's much wisdom in the old saying, "The longest journey begins with one small step." Break your goals down into small, manageable steps. Get help with this process if needed from someone who is good at this. This is where the linear planners excel!

Write it Down

Put your goal down in writing. Written commitments seem to carry more weight than ideas in your mind. When you put it in writing, your goal can also serve as a visual reminder for you. This will help you to follow though with your plan.

When writing your goal, rather than stating things in a negative fashion, try to state the goal more positively. Phrase it as a wish or a want. Rather than "Stop talking," write—"I wish that I would allow other people more time to talk."

216

EXERCISE

Goal Setting

Fill in the blank in the sentences below to put your goal in writing.

I want to _____.
(Remember: Just one at a time and worded positively)

Develop an Action Plan

An action plan is the list of steps you are going to take to get the results you want. It maps out a plan to meet your goal and serves as both a guide and management system. Professional athletes don't go into action without a game plan and neither should you. You will need behavior-change strategies to develop your game plan. Brainstorm different strategies that might help you meet your goal. How are you going to work on your goal? What are the steps involved?

Put together your plan in writing. This process helps to organize your thoughts, prompt ideas, and keep you on track. Written action plans keep the goal in focus.

Your action plan also needs a timeline. When will you do what? Is it doable? There is a tendency with AD/HD to have great intentions, but poorer follow-through. A timeline will hold you accountable and limit procrastination.

Evaluate Your Progress

Try charting your progress, especially if you are a visual person. Many people are encouraged by a graph which visually reminds them of how they're doing. It's the "You are here!" sign that keeps you oriented. Reviewing the graph can also help encourage you to go on when the going is tough.

So how are you doing? If your goal is clear and measurable, it will be easier to evaluate your progress. If you or others are having a difficult time determining whether or not you are making headway, your goal is probably too vague. Try to reword your goal for additional clarity if needed.

Are you able to make successful progress toward your goal? If so—keep going. If not, reevaluate your goal and your plan and make revisions. To use another old gambling cliché, "You gotta know when to hold 'em, and know when to fold 'em." If you've set an unreachable goal for yourself, there's no harm in chopping it down a bit. It would actually be wise to create smaller "baby steps" that are easier to accomplish.

Reward Yourself

Reward yourself for successes in meeting your goal. Don't just wait until the end! Reward yourself all along way. This should help provide the encouragement that you need to keep up the momentum.

JUST THE FACTS

- Look inward and determine where you are with regard to social skills.

- People you know can be a gold mine of information for you in discovering your blind side—if you just ask.

- Checklists are included in the Appendix to help assess your strengths and growth areas.

- Choose only one area to focus on at a time.

- Put your goal down in writing.

- Develop an action plan to list the steps you are going to take toward your goal.

- Keep track of your progress.

- Reward yourself for successes in meeting your goal. Reward yourself all along way.

NOTES

1. Yalom, I. (1975). *The theory and practice of group psychotherapy.* (4th ed.). New York: Basic Books, Inc. p. 490.

Chapter 12

Where Can I Go for Help?
Counseling and Doctors

"I'VE BEEN DEPRESSED as long as I can remember," said Hillary in her first counseling session with me. She was also seeing a psychiatrist, who gave her medication for the depression. But Hillary wasn't progressing well. Even with counseling, she still seemed bogged down by her failures and limitations.

Hillary's 17-year-old son also suffered from depression. During his treatment, it was discovered that he actually had AD/HD, predominately inattentive type. Hillary's son blossomed once he understood his diagnosis and was treated with medication and counseling for AD/HD. The focus then shifted back to Hillary.

Evaluating her own behavior, Hillary realized that she always had difficulty focusing her attention or retaining information. Through clinical interviews, the picture became clearer. Like her son, Hillary also had AD/HD. In fact, her depression was probably a result of her attentional difficulties.

Her treatment shifted to focus on AD/HD, and she began to make progress. Through the use of medication, paired with counseling, she began to understand her life of struggles.

221

As coping strategies were developed and implemented, she began to take new risks and dream new dreams. Hillary actually had the courage to return to college and pursue a career of her choice. The last I heard from her, she had graduated on the dean's list and was in an exciting new relationship.

AD/HD is serious business. It's not something that simply goes away if you ignore it, or if you try harder to pay attention, or if you change your diet. It has a physical cause in the brain, and its symptoms permeate throughout a person's life. But you don't have to face this problem on your own. There are professionals who are specifically trained to help you manage your AD/HD better.

Every so often you'll see a TV commercial that shows a car racing around a track, or weaving through cones, or stopping on a dime. This image of "high performance" is used to sell us a particular car or a brand of gas. But in the middle of these ads, fine print pops up: "Professional driver on a prepared track. Do not attempt these maneuvers." Or "Don't try this at home!"

I hope the ideas you read in this book will help you better manage various aspects of AD/HD—after all, this is a self-help book. Although there are a number of recommendations and suggestions you can follow by yourself, there are certain "maneuvers" that require professional skill. You will need outside help for certain aspects, such as diagnosis and medical management. And if you get stuck, you can probably benefit from outside help from a counselor or a coach to help you identify strategies to improve your social skills.

First, you need a proper ***diagnosis***. Do you actually have AD/HD? There are some other problems that mimic AD/HD, and you may have other difficulties *along with* AD/HD. With the right evaluation, a psychologist or psychiatrist can diagnose your situation accurately.

You may need ***medical management***. Certain medications can curb some symptoms of AD/HD, and these are prescribed by a medical doctor or psychiatrist. Medication won't solve all your problems, but it may help set the stage for success.

You may need ***counseling***. As you know, AD/HD affects many aspects of your life, and many emotional issues can arise. Like Hillary, who suffered from depression, many people need help with AD/HD-related issues. A trained counselor or psychologist can help you talk about these issues and can also help you develop strategies to better manage your AD/HD.

You may find ***behavior management*** useful. While this book and others can give you practical ideas on changing your lifestyle, you may benefit from the aid of professionals to help you develop your own personal strategies.

You may also benefit from the use of a ***coach***. A coach can help support you in developing and implementing strategies to meet your goals.

Diagnosis

Say your car's making a funny noise. You take it to your mechanic, who says, "Sounds like I'm going to have to rebuild your engine." Your mechanic does excellent work. He does an absolutely outstanding job on your engine. Sure, it costs you a bundle, and you have to go without transportation for a few days, but you know the rebuilt engine is better than new.

223

But the car still makes that noise. You take it back in, and your mechanic says, "Hmmmm. Must have been the transmission."

What's the problem? Did your mechanic do shoddy work? Not at all. He did a great job on the engine; he just didn't do so well on the diagnosis. He fixed the wrong thing.

Psychology can be like that, too. When I treated Hillary for depression, it wasn't working. Why not? The treatment should have worked—it had worked with many others who were depressed—but the diagnosis was wrong. Depression wasn't her main problem. Once we began treating the main problem—AD/HD—we began to make headway.

For many years, improper diagnosis was a very common story. People didn't know much about AD/HD. Some thought of it only as a children's problem. Since AD/HD regularly brings other problems along with it—depression, anxiety, learning disabilities, passive-aggressive behavior, even addiction—counselors were working on those problems rather than AD/HD.

Times have changed. People are more aware of adult AD/HD, but misdiagnosis still occurs. Those other problems are usually more obvious than AD/HD. Those are the things that bring you in for counseling, and so those are what the counselor tries to "fix." But AD/HD is often the underlying cause.

Such a combination of disorders is referred to as comorbidity. It's the job of the professional to determine which came first, the chicken or the egg—or in this case the depression or AD/HD. This process is known as differential diagnosis.

But sometimes the misdiagnosis can swing the other way. You might read a book like this and say, "That's it! That's my problem! I must have AD/HD!" You look at the symptoms—inattention, hyperactivity, impulsivity—yep, that's AD/HD, all right. You may be right or you may be wrong.

I've known people who started "diagnosing" others right and left. "That girl at the coffee shop, she's so hyper, she must have ADD. The guy at the theater is so spontaneous it's got to be ADD. My boss is so disorganized . . ." People need to be careful about such casual diagnosis.

Maybe those people do have AD/HD, but you can't make a proper diagnosis based on a messy desk. There are actually many other characteristics which can look like AD/HD to the untrained eye. At times AD/HD symptoms may be the result of another medical condition. So don't jump to conclusions. It's well worth the time, energy, and money to obtain a proper diagnosis from a professional with extensive experience in the area of AD/HD. However, not all professionals are equally experienced and talented. Check around to see who others have successfully used.

It is generally best to see a psychologist or psychiatrist for diagnosis. They are most familiar with the alternative psychological disorders that may mimic or accompany AD/HD. Some family physicians and neurologists also specialize in AD/HD and do an excellent job. Ask questions regarding the number of clients with AD/HD they treat. AD/HD can be complicated to diagnose so clinicians without training and expertise in this area may misdiagnose the problem.

Questions for Your Doctor

To help you select a professional, the following questions will be helpful in guiding you through a comparative process.[1] Usually the office personnel can provide you with the answers you need to make an informed decision.

1. Do you see a lot of clients with adult AD/HD? How many have you treated over the past year?
2. How long have you been working with adults with AD/HD?
3. What is involved in your assessment and treatment process? (Written tests? Interviews? Family history? Behavior modification? Medication?)
4. What are the costs involved?
5. Have you received any special training in the diagnosis or treatment of adult AD/HD? (They should have attended workshops/seminars, and/or read widely on the subject.)

The diagnosis for AD/HD is not made on the basis of any particular test. It is made from an evaluation process including a clinical interview, rating scales, observations, and sometimes actual testing such as an individual intelligence test or visual motor tests. This process is similar to that of diagnosing depression or anxiety disorders.

There are some doctors who are beginning to use brain scans to help in the diagnosis of AD/HD. This is definitely an interesting area to watch for future development, but not yet refined or readily available.

Medical Management

Once you have an official diagnosis, medical management can be considered. Proper medication in the right dosage can help a great deal. It's at least worth consideration.

We now know that AD/HD is a physiological disorder. The brain is not functioning properly. That's what causes all the problems in the areas of inattention, hyperactivity, and impulsivity. Fortunately, since AD/HD is a medical condition, it can be treated medically in most cases.

For medical management, choose a physician or psychiatrist with experience in the area of adult AD/HD to help you understand the treatment options, given your particular difficulties. There are still a number of doctors with very limited understanding of the medical treatment options available. Personal recommendations are a great source of information for locating a qualified physician in your area.

A variety of medications are used very successfully for adults with AD/HD. Adderall®, a stimulant, is growing in use with adults who have AD/HD. Concerta®—methylphenidate in a new once-a-day dosing delivery system which lasts twelve hours—is now available. Other medications include Ritalin®, Dexedrine®, Cylert®, Desoxyn®, Desipramine®, Effexor®, Imipramine®, Prozac®, Zoloft®, Luvox®, Wellbutrin®, and Clonidine®. In case one medication doesn't work for you, your doctor has several options to consider.

The advantage of medication is that it helps to restore the brain to a more "normal" mode of functioning. Although it's not a cure, it does help while it is being used. This brings up two points regarding medication, which are critical to improving interpersonal relationships.

But I don't want to take medication.

You may have interpersonal difficulties because you find it difficult to hold back impulsive comments, slow down the hyperactive movements, listen, or organize your life. Even with the best intentions, you may often fail to make improvements—frustrating yourself and others with your lack of progress. Sometimes it's important not just to work *harder*, but to work *smarter*.

John and Joyce had come to counseling because of marriage problems. Although they recently learned that Joyce had AD/HD, they decided against medication as a treatment option. Their marriage was falling apart, and they were considering divorce. Counseling was their last hope.

As they relayed their concerns and frustrations, it became clear that a number of AD/HD-related difficulties were creating havoc in their relationship. Joyce was not able to organize the house effectively. She was not able to meet the needs of their six children in anything close to an organized manner. There were many tears and frustrated words over forgotten children, undone laundry, unpaid bills, missed appointments and peanut butter and jelly sandwiches for dinner way too many times.

John was angry. If Joyce truly cared, he felt, she should be able to focus on the things that were important to him. After all, she was home full time while he went to work all day and put in long hours. Joyce had learned to shut down to avoid John's anger. She avoided him. They almost never did anything fun anymore. They were too overwhelmed with the basic activities of life.

Although Joyce had gained a basic understanding of AD/HD, and she really wanted to do better, she seemed unable to change her behavior. She would wake up with good intentions and fail before she even drank her coffee in the morning. Sometimes she had even forgotten to buy the coffee! She just wasn't able to try any harder and her life was falling apart.

After trying to implement some changes developed in counseling, without much success, Joyce decided to see if medication could help. Within the first few weeks of using medication, Joyce suddenly saw some changes. For the first time, her brain was actually allowing her to do what she wanted it to do. John noticed the improvement as well.

Over time her medication was adjusted to allow Joyce to function much more effectively. As a result Joyce was able to work on improving the areas that were causing her and her family such great concerns. Joyce was no longer depressed and overwhelmed with life. John was no longer frustrated and angry.

They still had to work on relationship issues, as well as strategies for coping with the difficulties that remained, but hope had been restored to their relationship.

Medication can set the stage for success. It can help you slow down, focus, stop, and think before speaking. Earlier I mentioned something my son Jarryd told me—that part of his brain must have been broken, the part that enables him to stop and think first. He was exactly right.

Medication can help your brain work better. It can set the stage for a major improvement in your social skills. Pills are not skills, but medication can prepare you to respond to others in a more socially appropriate manner.

But I don't want to take medication all the time.

You may already take medication. Perhaps you take it only when you're working. At home you may have decided to not use your medication. If this is a time when you have social difficulty, you may want to consider using your medication in social situations as well as work situations.

Some pediatricians used to (and a few still may) prescribe Ritalin® for children to be used only during the school day. However, in their off-hours, these same children often had difficulty with their homework and, even more importantly, their social relationships. It is now standard practice for physicians to prescribe medication to cover the full life of the child, not just school. A child's world is much more than just school performance. And your life is much more than your work.

Bob didn't want to take too much medication, so he used it sparingly. But he and his girlfriend had found that he was better able to listen and discuss important matters when he was using his medication. They developed a strategy that worked for them. If Bob's girlfriend had important issues to discuss with him, she'd ask him to take his medication a few hours earlier. That way he would be more attentive. But if they were just going to the movies, or hanging out, the medication wasn't necessary.

Some have found alternatives to medication, such as biofeedback, nutritional supplements, and dietary restriction helpful in managing AD/HD symptoms. To date, the research does not generally support these approaches, although there are a number of individual success stories. It's an area to watch.

Work together with your physician and those closest to you to determine your best medical treatment strategy. But please don't overlook the importance of social relationships when considering medication.

Counseling

Counseling comes in many different shapes and sizes, but it's not a "one size fits all" kind of thing. There are different counseling styles and different levels of training for those who call themselves counselors. Here's a brief overview to get you started.

What is Counseling?

Counseling is the process of talking with a trained professional to help you understand and work through your problems, which improves the quality of your life. Obviously, counselors are not limited to helping only with AD/HD concerns. Counselors can work with issues such as improving interpersonal relationships, depression, anxiety, poor self-esteem, anger management, problem solving, assertion training, addictions, conflict resolution skills, identification of learning styles (auditory vs. visual processors), facilitating personal growth, and behavior management.

There are several different forms of counseling. Counseling can be provided in an individual, couple, family, or group format. Each of these settings has a different emphasis. It's important for you to feel comfortable with your counselor/therapist and in the setting. Some people feel they benefit most from the attention of one-to-one individual counseling. Others find that feedback in a group is just what they need to help move them forward.

Finding the right match can be like trying on shoes. Find something that's comfortable. Sometimes, even though you thought that you made a good choice, after "wearing" it for a little, you realize that it was not such a good fit after all. One client I worked with had "tried on" 11 different counselors! Check with people you know and respect for counseling recommendations. Often this can help you narrow your search. You will be probably be involved in counseling for a while, so it's a good idea to find the right match.

Counseling can take anywhere from a few sessions to a few years. It usually varies depending on your issues and your rate of progress. The general orientation of the therapist also makes a difference regarding the length of counseling. For example, counselors with a psychodynamic orientation generally view counseling as more of a long-term process. Those with a cognitive-behavioral orientation see it as more short-term. So asking your counselor about his or her orientation, as well as the general length of treatment expected, will help you make an informed decision.

Counselor orientations also make a difference as to how the counselor will work with you. In general, AD/HD issues respond better to the structured format of a more cognitive-behavioral approach. Cognitive-behavioral therapy is more direct and more oriented toward problem solving than other approaches. Many counselors, however, effectively use a variety of therapeutic interventions to best address client needs.

Fees for counseling can vary, based on your location as well as the training and experience of your counselor. Ballpark figures range from $55 to $125 an hour for individual or marriage and family counseling, and $25 to $55 for group sessions. Some professionals provide a sliding scale based on financial need. Many counseling centers also provide a number of low-fee counseling slots for those with special needs. Counseling internship students, for example, often provide counseling for $10 a session (but remember that they have much less training and experience!). As one client told me, "Counseling is expensive, but it sure costs less than a divorce!"

Who Does What?

Counselor/Therapist: Actually these terms are the most general. Anyone can call themselves a "counselor" or a "therapist." These are not protected terms and there are no educational or experiential requirements. So be careful to check credentials. There is now certification for counselors through the National Board of Certified Counselors (NBCC). Check to see if your counselor is certified by NBCC. Counselors can be licensed in some states. Either certification or licensure is a good indication that they have been properly trained. They should at least have a master's degree in the field of counseling or some area of mental health.

Psychologist: This is a legally protected term and only those who meet stringent educational and experiential requirements can call themselves psychologists. A psychologist generally has a doctorate degree (Ph.D., Ed.D., or Psy.D.), or in some states a master's degree (M.A., M.S., M.Ed.), along with several years of experience. A psychologist is licensed by the state. Psychologists are trained in both diagnosis and counseling. Some also have expertise in behavior management.

Marriage and Family Therapist: Certified marriage and family therapists have at least a master's degree in addition to training and experience in working with couples and families. Some have made treatment of AD/HD couples and families a specialty area.

Social Worker: A social worker needs a master's degree to be licensed by the state. Be careful to check into their actual training, since some have had very little training and experience in counseling those with AD/HD. Of course there are always some who have made this their specialty area and do a great job. Social workers are generally not trained in diagnosis.

Psychiatrist: Psychiatrists are medical doctors (M.D.) who specialize in medical management. Some also provide counseling. Again, check to see if counseling is a specialty. Psychiatrists many actually have very little training and experience in counseling unless they have selected this as a specialty. They do however, excel in medical management and diagnosis.

Family Physician: General practitioners or family doctors have medical degrees (M.D. or D.O.) and are trained in basic diagnosis and treatment of a variety of disorders. Most are aware of their limitations and have an extensive referral network. A number have been known, however, to make inaccurate diagnoses—so beware. On the other hand, some have made adult AD/HD a specialty area and provide great treatment. If you are using a family doctor and it is working, stick with him or her. But if you're not making the progress you want, consider seeing someone with more expertise in this area.

Summary

If you're struggling with AD/HD symptoms, I recommend that you consider getting professional help. One of the pleasures of working in the field of AD/HD is that there are so many things that can be done to improve the quality of people's lives. People's lives can be dramatically transformed with proper treatment.

Please don't suffer needlessly. The right medication can set the stage for improvements you've been unable to accomplish on your own. Counseling can help you develop the insight and skills you've been missing.

Take care of yourself and your relationships. You're worth it. And the significant people in your life are worth it, too.

JUST THE FACTS

- There are professionals who are specifically trained to help you with AD/HD.

- Make sure you have an accurate diagnosis. Because AD/HD can be complicated to diagnose, misdiagnose can be a problem. Check around to see who others have successfully used.

- Fortunately, since AD/HD is a medical condition, it can be treated medically. There are a number of medications that are currently being used successfully to treat adults with AD/HD.

- Medication can set the stage for a major improvement in your social skills. Don't overlook the importance of social relationships in your medication strategy. Not using medication for social situations can sometimes have troubling results.

- There are different kinds of counseling styles and different levels of training for those who do "counseling."

- Counseling can be provided in an individual, couple, family, or group format.

- Counselors can help not only with AD/HD concerns, but also with a variety of other issues such as depression, anxiety, addictions, etc.

235

NOTES

1. Whiteman, T., & Novotni, M. (1995). *Adult ADD: A reader-friendly guide to identifying, understanding and treating adult attention deficit disorder.* Colorado Springs, Colorado: Pinion Press. p. 80.

Chapter 13

Who's on Your Team? Coaching

by Susan Sussman, M.Ed.
Master Certified Coach
A pioneer in the ADD coaching field, Susan is Director of the American Coaching Association. She engages in a full coaching schedule, conducts seminars and workshops, and consults with academic institutions and businesses.

Although it may seem new, the concept of coaching has been around for a long time. We are all familiar with athletic coaches, music teachers, mentors, and role models—all coaches. Coaching takes place in all aspects of life and is becoming increasingly popular in working with adults with AD/HD.

Coaching is both a partnership and a process aimed at helping you take steps towards achieving your vision, goals, or desires. A coach walks with you in your process of self discovery. In *The Wizard of Oz*, the "yellow brick road" led to Emerald City. Most people have their own "Emerald Cities"—destinations they want to reach. But sometimes, destinations become obscured. You may need some help in making the path more clear.

237

In the movie, Dorothy is the guide for the Tin Man, Lion, and Scarecrow. She coaches them to see their strengths and helps them realize they already have the qualities needed for success: a heart, courage, and a brain. The AD/HD coach, like Dorothy, can help you assess your strengths and weaknesses, work from your strengths, and learn new coping strategies in areas of weakness.

The focus of coaching can be on work, school, career planning, household duties, use of leisure time, or personal relationships. The primary goals of coaching are to help you to achieve a balanced lifestyle and to learn the skills that will enhance your functioning in various areas. The following is a list of some specific areas that you may work on with a coach.

- Appreciating the impact of AD/HD in your life
- Making choices
- Setting priorities
- Understanding how you learn and work best
- Evaluating and developing the skills needed to accomplish tasks
- Organizing tasks from the start
- Sustaining effort
- Discovering your personal roadblocks to success
- Developing an awareness of and appreciation for your unique potential[1]

A coach can be a valuable team member in helping you to improve your social skills. Coaches use of variety of tools and techniques to help you identify and stay on your path to success. The AD/HD coach provides support to help you develop the structure, strategies, and skills you need to reach your goals in social relationships and in other areas of your life.

The Four S's to Success: Support, Structure, Skills, and Strategies

Support

Everyone needs support. However, it is crucial for people with AD/HD, who have often spent years feeling blamed, criticized, and misunderstood. With AD/HD there is often a sense of isolation. Social support systems may be limited. Coaches provide a safe environment for you to tell your life story, to feel understood, to have someone empathize with you, and help you develop your goals. At times coaches may make referrals to therapists or physicians for additional support if needed.

Coaches are both supportive and yet emotionally neutral. They are not acting or reacting from their own emotional issues but rather from a professional desire to help you succeed. In most cases, working with a professional coach is more beneficial than using family members or people close to you. Other issues are often involved in those relationships. With coaching, "other stuff" doesn't get in the way. Often when those close to you try to offer support or help, it may be perceived as nagging, or you may be reluctant to share your difficulties. Coaches are trained to help you feel supported throughout the process.

Individuals with AD/HD can easily become distracted from their goals. Delaying immediate gratification is tough! "Individuals with AD/HD are often 'time blind'," writes Russell Barkley. "The only time that seems to exist for them is 'now." [2] Coaches help you understand your motivational patterns and help you design strategies to stay on task over time. They can be instrumental in helping you define your long-term goals, short-term objectives, and they provide support to help you stay focused on your goals.

Ken , a college student, liked to party. When faced with a choice between working on a paper or going to a party, Ken was unable to focus on his goals, dreams, and ambitions for the future. In that instant he was not focusing on writing the paper, passing the course, and graduating, so he could get a job, marry his girlfriend, and raise a family. In that instant, he just wanted to have fun. Ken had trouble focusing on the future.

Through coaching, Ken was encouraged to create a "dream board," which is a collage made by gluing photographs and pictures from magazines onto cardboard. Ken created a collage of an attractive house with kids playing on the lawn, himself at the barbecue, and his girlfriend working in the garden. He placed his "dream board" next to his computer as a reminder to help him stay focused on the alternative to partying.

Because self-care is often overlooked, coaches also encourage you to take care of and support yourself. AD/HD symptoms can become more pronounced during times of stress and fatigue, which often result from an absence of self care. Coaching can help you understand the impact diet, sleep habits, and exercise programs have on your life. Paying attention to *lifestyle* issues in coaching helps you learn to safeguard your own well-being.

In *Emotional Intelligence*, Daniel Goleman discusses the importance of an aspect of self care he refers to as "self-soothing"—the ability to bounce back from life's stressors.[3] Coaching offers clients an opportunity to develop a repertoire of self-soothing strategies and techniques.

Wayne, a computer whiz, who worked at home debugging programs for his clients, was often glued to the computer for long hours. This often left him cranky when he had time to spend with his wife and children. In addition, his work pattern seemed to precipitate migraine headaches. In coaching conversations it was discovered that Wayne liked jazz, walking, and taking a long bath, all of which he felt that he just didn't have time for.

Through coaching Wayne decided to restructure his workday to reduce the prolonged stretches at the computer. Wayne's plan involved creating three intensive 2-hour work sessions broken up by two 45 minute breaks (one for walking and one for jazz). His new schedule ended his day with a bath, providing a soothing transition from his workday to his home life. As a result of attending to self-soothing, Wayne had fewer migraine headaches and was much less irritable around the important people in his life.

Structure

Structure, planning, and organization are important factors in everyone's life, but perhaps even more so for individuals with AD/HD. Without structure, you may feel at the mercy of the winds, blown about like a rudderless ship—*reactive*. With structure, you can craft your days and destinies, chart your own course on life's seas and become *proactive*. In *The Seven Habits of Highly Effective People*, Steven Covey writes about the importance of setting goals and then creating structure in your daily life that will allow you to reach those goals.[4]

Your coach can help you craft a structure that will meet your short-term obligations and move toward long-term goals in a *pro-active* rather than a *reactive* manner. People with

241

AD/HD are often hard-wired to be reactive—responding to the loudest, brightest, newest, or most exciting thing in their environment. Nancy Ratey, a leader in the ADD coaching field, says that it's especially important to "engineer" environments to minimize distractions and interruptions.

Lisa, a news reporter, was almost always late with her stories. She constantly had her editor on her back. This created an atmosphere of high anxiety and strained relation-

ships around the office. Prior to coaching, it hadn't occurred to Lisa that she could have the office manager hold her phone calls for three hours every day giving her uninterrupted writing time. With the help of her coach, she also created a checklist that included items like checking her sources, doing research, and getting background material. By following a sequence of steps in putting her stories together and by structuring her environment to support her writing, Lisa was able to become proactive rather than reactive. With this structure, Lisa became more effective and her relationship with her editor improved significantly.

Skills

People with AD/HD are often inconsistent (a fact that is hard for parents, teachers, employers, and spouses to understand). One day they perform well; the next they can't. Because of this inconsistency, the world of those with AD/HD is not always predictable. Your reality can feel like a kaleidoscope, ever-changing, and random. You never know how your memory is going to work, or if you'll be able to concentrate. Will you be too distracted to focus on that project that's due later in the week? Will you remember how to use that new device your boss showed you? With such inconsistency as a regular companion, individuals with AD/HD need to work on building some solid life skills.

Usually "skill building" refers to tasks such as learning to fix a car or play a musical instrument. But in the coaching context, skill building means developing routines and rituals. You may be frequently late because you have difficulty deciding how to get ready each morning. What should you do first? Shower, eat breakfast, walk the dog, make coffee, brush your teeth, exercise or read the paper? With all those decisions to make, just getting out of the house can be exhausting!

243

Rather than having to make decisions each step of the way, coaching can help you develop the skill of creating routines. If all those items can be completed in the same order each day, they can almost be viewed as one large task. With automatic routines, life can become less inconsistent and therefore more predictable and easier.

Sometimes help is also needed to develop or improve a specific skill. For example, if you now realize that you need to improve your body language when you interact with others, a coach can help you find, develop, and practice those specific skills in a safe environment.

Strategies–The How

Jane was attractive and well-spoken, but when she wasn't at work, she was usually alone. Because of her inability to keep up with regular home maintenance, Jane didn't bring friends to her home. She had piles everywhere—clothes, books, papers, dishes, laundry, old furniture that needed to be discarded. What Jane wanted most from coaching was to develop systems for managing her "stuff" in a way that would allow her to engage in the give and take of friendship.

With coaching, Jane was able to develop strategies that worked for her. More importantly, she was able to create and maintain a home environment that she was proud of.

Strategies are the tools coaches use to help individuals learn new ways to achieve success. Learning new strategies for handling old difficulties can be exciting, challenging and rewarding. It requires a willingness to go from "automatic pilot" to the thoughtful approach used by seasoned navigators.

Individuals with AD/HD need to learn to reframe their ideas of the characteristics that are usually considered defi-

244

cits. For example, the hyperactive person who learns self-management strategies might become"energetic" rather than "antsy." He might be able to do this by:

- exercising before he got to work;
- keeping nutty putty and a spring-loaded hand exerciser at his desk that can be used quietly to release physical tension;
- taking a walk at lunch time; or
- keeping some upbeat music playing in the background.

The "impulsive" individual might develop strategies to become merely "spontaneous." How? By creating a space for reflection between a stimulus and its response. She might be able to do this by setting her countdown wrist watch to give her 60 seconds to reflect before reacting to a thought. During this time she asks herself only one question: "What would the consequences of this action be?" Learning to ask herself this one question routinely will help her anticipate what *could* go wrong *before the fact* rather than having to evaluate what *did* go wrong afterward.

This new language helps develop a new and more positive self image in both your mind as well as the perceptions of others.

How Does Coaching Work?

Coaching requires a readiness and willingness to make a commitment to yourself. Coaching requires that you invest your time, energy, and efforts to work toward your goals.

Coaching is provided in a variety of formats: phone, e-mail, and in person. Some coaches have regularly scheduled meetings each week, while others provide a variety of contact options.

Coaching costs vary, but in general fall somewhere between the fees charged by professional organizers and psychotherapists. Low cost coaching options may be available through the coach training organizations listed below.

Since national guidelines are not in place yet for the training of AD/HD coaches, backgrounds and experience vary. Some have been through training provided by one of the AD/HD coach training organizations listed below. Some come from allied backgrounds such as psychotherapy, education, professional organizing or medicine. Others have participated in a general coach training program that prepares people to be personal and professional coaches who do not specialize in AD/HD. The bottom line is that you need to ask about your prospective coach's training and background.

AD/HD Coach Training Organizations

Below are a list of organizations and resources that provide valuable information about adult ADHD, coaching, and products or services that may be helpful for those with ADHD.

American Coaching Association
Director: Susan Sussman, M.Ed., MCC
P.O. Box 353
Lafayette Hill, PA 19444
Phone: 610-825-4505

Optimal Functioning Institute
Founder/CEO: Madelyn Griffith-Haynie
Director: David Giwerc, B.S.
e-mail: support@addcoach.com
Phone: 518-482-3458

ADD BRAIN WORKS
Director: Nancy Ratey, Ed. M., MCC
264 Grove Street
Wessesley, MA 02181
Phone: 617-237-3508
www.addbrain.com

ADD Consults
Director: Terry Matlen, MSW, ACSW
www.addconsults.com

Catalytic Coaching
Director: Sandy Maynard
1722 19th Street NW #508
Washington, D.C. 20009
Phone: 1-888-REFRAME
www.sandymaynard.com

Conclusion

Coaching is a forum for learning. A safe place to try on new behaviors. A map for the lost traveler on the "yellow brick road".

A coach can:
- help you make desired changes in your life;
- provide accountability and hold your agenda;
- help you understand your strengths and weaknesses;
- empower you;

In *Driven to Distraction*, Edward Hallowell and John Ratey summarized it well when they said, "Coaching can offer hope." [5]

JUST THE FACTS

- Coaching is a forum in which social skills can be developed and practiced.

- Coaches help clients identify and stay on the path to success.

- Coaches are supportive and help you develop skills, strategies, and structure.

- Coaching fees, format and training varies.

NOTES

1. Kelly, K. ADDed Dimension Coaching website. www.addcoaching.com.
2. Barkley, R. (1997) *ADHD and the nature of self-control.* New York: Guilford Press.
3. Goleman, D. (1995) *Emotional intelligence.* New York: Bantam Books.
4. Covey, S. (1989) *The 7 habits of highly effective people.* New York: Simon Schuster.
5. Hallowell, E., & Ratey, J. (1994) *Driven to distraction.* New York: Pantheon Books.

Chapter 14

How Can I Change?
Behavior Management

EVERY DAY, PEOPLE go on diets. Perhaps they're unhappy with their weight, or maybe they just want to be healthier. In any case, they've decided that they haven't been eating right, and it's time to change. So they work at developing new eating habits. No more hot fudge sundaes. Lots more celery.

That's behavior management. It's not easy. It requires commitment, willpower, patience, and persistence. If you've ever tried to quit a bad habit such as smoking or start a good habit such as exercising, you know the challenge of behavior management.

In most cases, for folks with AD/HD, behavior is the problem. Whether you're always fidgeting in business meetings, talking incessantly, or losing your keys, it's your behavior that frustrates you and gets you into trouble with others. Sure, you'll need willpower, but you'll need more than that. You'll need a strategy.

Behavior management strategies can be quite effective in helping you reorder your life and improve your social relationships. This chapter offers you some tactics that have helped many in managing AD/HD symptoms. You can try

249

on your own (practice exercises are included), or find a professional to help you identify and apply the behavioral strategies that might work best for you.

Verbal Prompts

Jarryd can overwhelm me at times with all of his talking, especially when I first come home from work. Usually I'm tired and trying to get dinner on the table. One of the strategies that has been helpful is to cue him with a verbal prompt. "Jarryd, I need a pause. My brain can't quite keep on going." Fortunately, he's generally responsive to that prompt and will give me the much needed quiet.

Sometimes the first prompt doesn't work. And sometimes he'll say, "Do you really think that I'm talking too much? I don't think that I'm talking too much. I know sometimes I do talk too much, but not now, I'm not talking too much. Am I? Am I?" And I have to remind him not to argue, but just to listen to those prompts. He then zips up his mouth.

Using verbal prompts also works outside of the home. One of the strategies we taught Jarryd to use with his friends was to tell them, "Look, I have ADD and one of the problems is that sometimes I talk too much. I really don't want to, and I don't know when I'm doing it. Would you please tell me when I'm talking too much and then I'll shut up." So he has actually trained his friends to prompt him when he talks too much. And they'll just say, "Jarryd, shut up." For now, this has been helpful because even on medication, he still is sometimes unaware of when he is talking too much or "speed talking." At times, he really does need that prompt to slow down and give others a chance to talk.

Verbal prompts can be a very powerful strategy for those coping with AD/HD. It is best for those giving the prompts to be thoughtful and considerate. Kind prompts are actually much better than *shut up!* Softer comments like "Sorry, I just can't listen anymore" or "I need a pause" would work. See "20 Tips for Those Who Want to Help" in the Appendix.

Gestural Prompts

Say you're at a party with a friend and you're starting to go off on an AD/HD tangent. Your friend notices, but doesn't want to publicly embarrass you. If they wait till later to tell you, you'll leave the folks at the party with a bad impression of you.

But what if, in advance, you worked out some type of gesture to let you know that your conversation or behavior is off? When you're having an AD/HD moment, your friend can pull at an ear, scratch their head, or sneeze. The gesture can flag you to adjust your behavior before you embarrass yourself, but no one will know the gesture except you and your friend. Be creative in setting up the gesture. You want something natural, but hard to miss.

EXERCISE

Using Gestural Prompts

1. Ask someone to help you to work on a specific social skill that you have selected.
2. With this person, develop a gestural prompt that will give you the signal that you may need.
3. Go into a social situation and try it out.
4. Evaluate whether or not it was helpful.
5. If it was helpful, use it again. If not, figure out what went wrong and work out the kinks.

Physical Prompts

Sometimes a physical prompt from someone, such as a gentle touch on the arm, can also be effective in alerting you to a social error. Be subtle. Bops on the head or jabs in the ribs are a bit too obvious.

There are even gadgets that can provide you with physical prompts. Vibrating watches can be set to go off at certain times, keeping you on track socially. For instance, if you are going to be at a party and you know that you often talk too much, you can set your vibrating watch to go off at five-minute intervals. If you're talking when the watch vibrates, quickly finish up and ask the others questions. The watch is saying, "Be quiet for a while." Or if you talk too fast, it can be a reminder to slow down. This physical prompt would not be noticed by others, can be self-regulated, and should help you remember whatever you want to remember.

QUICK TIP

Consider getting a vibrating watch to use as a physical prompt for you.

Visual Cues

Perhaps a visual cue can serve as a reminder for you. Sometimes a forgetful person will wear a rubber band around a wrist, write a word on their hand, or place an item within their view to help them remember. Using the same example as above, perhaps you could wear a rubber band or a special bracelet around your wrist. Then, every time you see the rubber band or bracelet, it should cue you to remember to stop talking and allow others to talk.

Sticky notes can be great visual cues. Many clients have covered their bathroom mirror and car with such reminders. Many with AD/HD prefer the brightly colored notes because they grab your attention. Put reminders where you can't ignore them, and be specific about what they mean. Be creative in providing yourself with visual cues that meet your needs.

EXERCISE

Visual Cues
1. Choose a social skill.
2. Select a visual cue that should help you remember to work on the skill.
3. Go into a social situation and try it out.
4. Evaluate the effectiveness of your visual cue. If it worked, use it again. If not, develop a new visual cue.

Properly done, subtle prompts—whether visual, verbal or physical—can all steer you away from trouble without embarrassment. Some are well-suited for you to use independently; some require the assistance of others. Don't be shy about asking friends to prompt you. They may enjoy the opportunity to help, and with pre-arranged cues, it can be fun.

Environmental Strategies

In behavior management, there are basically two areas that you can work on—the front end or the back end. You can change what happens *before* the problem behavior occurs (antecedents) or you can change what happens *after* the problem behavior occurs (consequences). Different approaches are suited for different behaviors.

253

On the front end, you rearrange your environment to try to keep problems from occurring. The point is, sometimes you find yourself in situations where you function well. At other times, the surroundings bring out all your worst AD/HD symptoms. If you can keep yourself in the good situations, and transform the bad ones, you'll go a long way toward effectively managing your behavior.

"An once of prevention is worth a pound of cure." That familiar saying applies here. If you take a proactive stance, changing your environment rather than just reacting to it, you can set the stage for success.

When Jarryd was little, he frequently forgot things. Life became very stressful each winter when we couldn't find his hat, gloves, or even his coat. When Jarryd was in the first grade, he really, really wanted a special winter coat. On sale, the coat still cost almost $100. Considering all the clothing he lost, this didn't seem to be a smart buy. But since he was in charge of managing his clothing money, I let him make the choice. Of course I pointed out that he only had $300 to spend on clothes for the whole year, and he might lose this expensive coat, but it was his decision. And he bought it.

Now I hoped he might take better care of the coat, since he wanted it so much. That was the whole idea of letting him decide, so he would become more responsible with his clothing. But do you want to guess how long Jarryd had his new coat before he lost it?

He lost it on the first day! Jarryd came home from school without his new coat the very first day he wore it. We quickly went back to the school playground where he last remembered having it, but his coat was gone. He was very disappointed.

That's when we decided to manipulate the environment to better accommodate his AD/HD. We went to a local thrift shop and bought him five $10 coats. Life became much easier at home with several coats and extra pairs of gloves and hats. We would never again be in the position of not having a coat on a cold morning—way too much stress. If he lost one, he had another. So this problem was no longer a problem.

Many of my clients have been in similar stressful situations, losing important items, such as the keys to their car or house. Rather than put yourself in a vulnerable position, it's better to prepare in advance for these problems. One dollar can buy you a spare key—heck, splurge and buy five! Put an extra key in your desk at work and at home. And maybe even put one under your car with one of those magnets. House keys can also be strategically hidden and/or given to neighbors. Any of these environmental manipulations eliminate the problem of a lost key.

Forgotten medication can also cause difficulties. But this can be easily remedied. Keep extra bottles of medication strategically located throughout your car, home, and workplace.

If you worry that you might embarrass yourself socially with hyperactivity or impulsive comments, alert a few key people in advance. Call your hosts or your teacher or your group leader ahead of time and explain that you have AD/HD and you might talk too much or move around a lot. Give them some verbal or visual prompts to help curb your behavior if it becomes a problem. Now, instead of attributing your behavior to rudeness or selfishness, they'll know what's going on. You'll be surprised how much they'll appreciate being forewarned. They might even make some additional accommodations.

At the beginning of the school year, I had a graduate student come to me, explaining that he had AD/HD with hyperactivity. He just wanted to give me a "heads up" that he might have to move around a lot in my class. He would try not to be disruptive. He asked me not to think that he was rude or bored—it was just AD/HD. I appreciated his forewarning. He was pleasantly surprised when I said it would be perfectly acceptable for him to get up and leave the classroom during class if he needed a stretch. He hadn't even considered that as an option!

EXERCISE

The Front End

1. Make a list of some of the problems your AD/HD causes in your life.
2. Determine which items on your list lend themselves to front end changes.
3. Select one and change the environment so that the problem is not as much of a problem.
4. If successful, pick another problem on your list and come up with another change. If it wasn't successful, figure out what went wrong and try again.

Prepare yourself for the environment

Another way to work with the front end of a problem behavior is to better prepare yourself for potential difficulties. If you know you'll be entering a problematic social situation, try to figure out what your difficulties are most likely to be. Then come up with an action plan. What can you do to avoid or lessen the difficulty? Practice your responses. (You mightfind it helpful to ask someone with better social skills to work with you, or consider using a coach or psychologist.)

Modeling

We can learn social skills by watching the behavior of others. Watch what others are doing in those situations that give you difficulty. Try to copy their behavior.

In a scene from the movie *Pretty Woman*, the character played by Julia Roberts was in a very fancy restaurant and uncertain of how to proceed with the many pieces of silverware in front of her. She didn't know, so she watched the others at her table for clues and then copied their behavior. That's modeling, and you can do it in any number of social situations.

EXERCISE

Modeling

1. Find someone who is able to demonstrate the social skill you're having trouble with. (If you can't find a model in real life, consider a television character.)

2. Watch him/her as many times as possible.

3. Try the skill yourself, keeping in mind how he/she would do it. Act as if you are that person when you are practicing the skill.

Role Play

Sometimes it's helpful to practice the social skill you are trying to develop. This practice is called role play. You'll need someone to act out certain situations with you. Perhaps this person will pretend to be your boss as you practice responding to criticism. Or pretend to interview you for a job. Think of the situation that gives you trouble and act it out.

Role play is a great way to get the kinks out of your behavior in a safe setting. It is much less threatening to practice your skills with a safe person, knowing that you have a number of opportunities to get it right. And when the time comes, if you have already role-played the situation successfully a number of times, you'll be much more confident in trying out your new skill.

EXERCISE

Role Play

1. **Find someone** to work with you on practicing a social skill.
2. **Set the stage**: tell the person the skill you want to work on and give him/her some ideas as to settings or circumstances that generally give you trouble.
3. **Action**: role play the situation for as long as you like. Try to pretend that you are actually talking to your boss or whoever the person is pretending to be.
4. **Ask for feedback**. Get his/her opinion of how you did and suggestions for improvement.
5. **Practice** again, implementing any changes.
6. **Repeat** until you are able to demonstrate the new skill with confidence.

Generalization through Visualization

Generalization means that what you learn in one setting you are also able to use in other similar settings. This is a challenge for many with AD/HD. You might have learned a particular social skill in one context, but you have a hard time carrying it over to another.

I ran a group for adults with AD/HD and part of the group time was devoted to teaching and practicing social skills. While in the group, the members were very focused on demonstrating the appropriate social skills. If, for example, we were working on not interrupting others, they were all pretty good at not interrupting during our practice sessions.

When we would take a break or end for the night, it was always troubling that it seemed they couldn't remember what they had just learned. I would see them interrupting all over the place. This is a lack of generalization—the inability to take a skill and use it successfully at another time or in another setting.

I had also found this to be true in working with Jarryd. He had learned some social skills—we had worked on them together—but once he was actually in a social situation, he often didn't use these skills. Or sometimes he would use the skill in one setting but not another where it was needed.

In trying to help Jarryd learn to apply his skills across settings, I had him practice his skills in a variety of situations. Generalization improves if a skill can be taught and reinforced in a variety of settings and circumstances.[1] This, however, was not always possible. And even when we practiced the skills a number of times in different settings, he still had a hard time transferring his knowledge to real life.

Frustrated with his lack of progress, I began searching for alternative methods. There wasn't much helpful research available on the subject, so we were pretty much on our own. I remembered using visualization in my doctoral program to teach assertion skills. In fact, a colleague of mine had done a dissertation comparing behavioral rehearsal with visualization training. Both had proven effective. Maybe this was the answer I'd been looking for.

So, in addition to the actual role-play situations, I asked Jarryd to visualize himself in a similar situation. "Don't actually say or do anything, just visualize it in your mind." Fortunately, he was able to do this. I asked him to tell me what he said and did in his visualization. I gave him feedback regarding appropriate social behavior. He then practiced the same situation several times in his mind.

Once he was able to demonstrate successful social skills in his visualization, I asked him to try the same skill but this time with a new person in mind. Again, I asked him to tell me what he said and did in this visualization. We reviewed any difficulties and practiced it again several times.

Using this method, we were able to practice his social skills many times in a number of "actual" settings with a number of the "actual" people he would be dealing with. This approach greatly improved his ability to generalize—to use his new skills in a variety of situations.

Taking what I had learned from working with Jarryd, I recommended visualization training to a number of clients to help improve their social skills. Some were very successful using this approach. In fact, this is actually one of the most successful techniques that I've found in helping people learn to apply social skills. However, some are unable to visualize or to stay focused on the visualization, so it doesn't work for everyone.

260

EXERCISE

Visualization

1. Select a social skill.
2. Imagine yourself actually using the appropriate social skill.
3. If you have someone to help you, go over what you said and did in your visualization. Get feedback. If you are doing this alone, evaluate yourself.
4. Do the visualization again, making any desired changes.
5. Evaluate again.
6. Practice at least five times.
7. Using visualization, practice this same skill with another person or another setting in mind.
8. Repeat the above steps.

The Back End

So far, we've been talking about the "front end" of your behavior, preparing the environment or yourself *before* the behavior occurs. Another strategy involves manipulating the back end—dealing with the consequences *after* the fact.

Unfortunately, many people want to jump right to punishment as a back-end intervention. However, the problem with punishment is that it doesn't teach correct behaviors. It just lets you know what not to do.

When Jarryd was little, he would be placed in "time out" for a variety of inappropriate behaviors. After he did something wrong, such as trying to hit his brother, he was sent to the hallway steps for a few minutes to think about what he had done and what he should have done instead. Following time out, we would discuss better options. Because Jarryd was very hyperactive and impulsive, he went to time out a lot in the early years. He came to understand the process well— maybe too well.

Once he just came up to me and said, "I'm just going to time out now, mom. You don't have to worry about it." When I asked him what he had done wrong, he wouldn't tell me. He went over, sat on the hallway steps a few minutes, and then got up. I never found out what he had done.

And I don't know if he learned what to do instead. You see, punishment doesn't teach appropriate behavior. Reinforcement is a much more effective way to go about learning social skills. By rewarding positive behavior, you increase it. And increased positive behavior replaces undesirable behavior. Besides, the social rejection that usually occurs with social skill errors is punishment enough for anyone.

Rewards

Learn to reward yourself periodically for successful behavior. Think about what you like and what makes you happy. Then plan to indulge in those things if you behave properly in a difficult situation.

For example, you're in a meeting at work and successfully curtail your own talking, allowing others to speak. Good for you! Then celebrate that evening, renting a favorite video, going out to dinner, or taking a luxuriant bubble bath.

Or suppose you and your spouse need to have an important discussion, but you've been having a hard time staying focused. Maybe he or she will agree to give you a backrub if you succeed in paying attention during the discussion.

A variety of things can be used as reinforcers. It is not a good idea to always use the same reinforcer, because you will probably get tired of it. You may find different things to be reinforcing at different times in your life. Reinforcers generally fall into the categories of: food, activities, tangible items, and social reinforcers.

- **Food** might include: a candy bar, peanuts, steak, an ice cream cone.

- **Activities** include: a visit to the movies, getting a manicure or massage, a museum trip, a park outing, playing tennis or golf, eating out.

- **Tangible items** include any valued gifts such as jewelry, tools, sports equipment, video, CD, or money.

- **Social reinforcers** include hugs, smiles, verbal praise, and most importantly, being included.

    See what motivates you the most.

EXERCISE

Reinforcers
Finding Reinforcers:
1. Make a list of 10 possible *food* reinforcers for you.
2. Make a list of 10 *activity* reinforcers for you.
3. Make a list of 10 *items* that would be reinforcing for you.
4. Make a list of 10 *social* reinforcers for you.
5. Now using these lists, pick your top 10 reinforcers.

Using Reinforcers:
1. Select one social skill that you want to work on.
2. Select a reinforcer from your top 10.
3. Go into a social situation and use your social skill.
4. Reinforce yourself as planned!

Behavioral Shaping

In the movie *What about Bob?*, the title character used a concept called "baby steps" to help him work on his goal. Bob changed his behavior by focusing on just little steps rather than the big picture. "Baby steps" is known in the behavior management world as *behavioral shaping*, where small victories are rewarded, setting the stage for overall success.

Some people want to only reward perfect behavior. Stay out of that trap. Recognize improvements. Often the skill you're working on has several parts or even degrees of mastery. It would be very unlikely for you to get it perfectly right the first time. And if you wait until you have it perfect before you receive any encouragement, you may get discouraged in the process.

But if you reward small steps of improvement, you'll be encouraged. Over time, you can raise the bar, requiring more improvement before you reward yourself. You'll eventually be able to do the entire behavior well. But for now, focus on the "baby steps."

EXERCISE

Behavior Shaping

1. Identify a social skill you want to work on.
2. Identify several steps to get you from where you are to where you want to be.
3. Go into a social situation and try to use your new skill.
4. Reinforce yourself if you complete the first step.
5. Repeat a few times, then move on to include the next step.
6. Continue until you can successfully complete the social skill to the desired level.
7. If unsuccessful, identify what went wrong. Was the skill too hard? Do you need more steps? Do you need more practice before trying again? Is your reward not reinforcing enough?
8. Revise as needed and try again.

Instant Replay

On the back end, it's also important to understand what you did wrong when a social error has occurred. You cannot learn to act differently unless you understand what you did incorrectly.

Maybe you just got a weird reaction from people around you. (Take a moment to applaud yourself for *noticing* the weird reaction and understanding subtext and body language.) Replay the scene in your mind. *Who just said what? Who just did what?* See if you can discover where things went wrong.

Richard Lavoie calls this process of examination and reflection a "social autopsy." He has everyone use these autopsies regularly in the school he runs for children with learning disabilities. He helped them understand what just happened and what they need to do differently next time.[2]

If you are unable to uncover the difficulty or social error by yourself, ask someone who was there to help you. *I noticed that everyone seemed to go away from the group I was in. Was I doing something wrong? What happened?*

When you ask for help in understanding a situation, be open to hearing what the person has to say. Remember: if the others have good social skills and you're having social difficulties, their understanding of the situation is likely to be more accurate than yours. Try to see things from another perspective.

JUST THE FACTS

- Behavior management strategies can be quite effective in helping those with AD/HD improve social relationships

- Properly done, subtle prompts—whether visual, verbal or physical—can all steer you away from trouble without embarrassment.

- In behavior management, there are basically two areas you can work on—the front end or the back end. You can change what happens *before* the problem behavior occurs or you can change what happens *after* the problem behavior occurs.

The Front End

- Prepare the environment. Change your environment to help you be more successful.

- Prepare yourself for the environment through modeling (copying the behavior of others) and role playing (practicing the social skill).

- To improve generalization (using the skill in different situations), use visualization by practicing the situation in your mind.

The Back End

- Rewards are important to provide encouragement in learning and keeping new skills.

- Use behavior shaping and reward yourself for successful "baby steps."

- Use the instant replay approach to figure out what went wrong.

NOTES

1. Miltenberger, R. (1997). *Behavior modification: Principles and procedures.* Pacific Grove, California: Brooks Cole Publishing Company. pp.267-284
2. Lavoie, R. (1994) *Learning disabilities and social skills: Last one picked...first one picked on.* Washington, D. C.: WETA-TV.

Part Five

Conclusion

Chapter 15

Words from the Trenches: Conclusion

I WOULD LIKE to thank the many people at the ADDIEN (ADDult Information Exchange Network) conferences in San Francisco, California (1999) and Ann Arbor, Michigan (1999), who shared their insights on the following three questions. (Their names were not included to protect their identities).

What social skill areas seem to cause you the most trouble?

Sometimes you can do something and get away with it and sometimes you can't. For instance, sometimes I can interrupt and my wife doesn't hit me in the ribs, or I can interrupt and nobody's facial expression changes. Eating with your mouth open is similar. My wife's cousin—if you ask him a yes-no question when he's chewing, he won't answer you. All it needed was a simple yes or no. He'll continue to chew for 10 to 15 seconds while everyone waits, swallow, and then finally say yes. Isn't there a time when you can say something with your mouth full? Isn't there a time when you can interrupt? It's very confusing!

271

***

Talking too much and disjointed ideas/topics (disjointed to others that is). I call it "Chain-talking" and "string-thinking." The thoughts may seem disjointed to others, but since the subjects to me are related, I see the connection.

***

One person wrote this in a letter:

I have difficulty remembering the details that crowd in and out of my mind like beads of mercury on top of water, going where THEY will, not where I need them to go! My word processor doesn't like the word ADDult (a term for Adult with AD/HD). It redlined it twice now. It's funny how a word processor's actions can mimic real life sometimes! Other people in my world don't like that word either. They probably wish that redlining it would make the disorder disappear as well—and then everything would be, well, normal. (Hey, then I wouldn't have to deal with it either!) However, the truth is it DOES exist. I know they would like to THINK that it doesn't exist—and as a result they almost come close to thinking that I don't exist either—that is, as an adult with ADD. My point is that adults with ADD, just like other people, like to be seen as "normal" but with a disability that needs to be taken into consideration—especially how it affects the hours of our lives, the spirit of our souls. It is THIS that I want to convey here—the real-life challenges and successes that are part of being an ADDult!

***

Telephone behavior causes me trouble because I have AD/HD and LD. I rely a lot on facial expressions and phone conversations seem detached, like a floating voice. So I avoid phone calls and hurt myself by not returning or delaying phone calls.

***

Keeping track of time always seems to get me in trouble.

***

Excerpts from a letter:

Here are some thoughts of mine on ADD and socializing, which I feel are important. I hope it's helpful and relevant.

I wanted to tell you about how socializing is work. Most well adjusted people do their best to balance the percentage of time they spend working and relaxing or recreating. Further, it is usually best not to play at work or work when you are supposed to be relaxing; that tends to ruin both activities. Most people put socializing in the "play" category; it's relaxing and recreational. People with ADD have to put out so much effort to socialize, it ends up in the "work" category. It's not relaxing at all. And it's usually unsuccessful, which leads to frustration, depression, "I must be a loser," etc. Because it requires so much effort, someone with ADD will work most of the week and if they try to do the psychologically healthy thing and engage in some well rounded social activity, they have to work some more. Leaving no time for relaxation or recreation. No wonder we're always exhausted.

273

I remember, reading about ADD, that the author said that we see life as an uphill battle and that all tasks seem overwhelming and require tremendous effort. I am now beginning to understand that all tasks ARE overwhelming and life IS an uphill battle. The language that we "see" life as an uphill battle, that tasks "seem" overwhelming is degrading. This type of language contributes to the concept that we are lazy, that we are somehow less than moral because we supposedly "choose" not to try.

According to most psychological models, socializing is required to be healthy. Well, it's difficult at best for people with ADD, nearly impossible for some. Some have given up trying, due to repeated failures; others continue to bang their heads against the wall. The undiagnosed are still wondering what is wrong or why other people can do this or that and I can't.

***

Even before I knew I had ADD, I was the kind of person who always "told it like it is." I guess that's one of the reasons that I found out that I had ADD. I'm going to tell you the truth. Once my sister-in-law bought my son a work bench for Christmas. The problem was that he already had one. So when I saw the gift, she asked me, "Do you like it?" I thanked her for the gift and told her that he already had one. She blew up. She refused to speak to me and that incident ruined our Christmas.

I'm more thoughtful now before I speak. I don't "tell it like it is" as hurtfully anymore because I now realize that I was hurtful in ways that I spoke.

***

274

I've been married a couple of times and I think that ADD has something to do with that. I'm a teacher and a coach and have been told that I have really good social skills with my clientele. In fact, I was told that I have outstanding social skills with my clientele. However, in a home situation, I was severely criticized for what was called my "free fall." I sort of call it "going with the flow." I think that it does get me into trouble. I sort of have a way of rolling with the punches. It's that old spontaneity thing. If you live with a planner, especially an obsessive planner, they don't take very kindly to that. It does cause problems. The two things that he couldn't tolerate about me were my "free fall" and that I had to be passionate about everything. That really bothered him. For instance, I wanted to get my kids in the right school to meet their educational needs. I felt passionately about that. Helping my clients—I felt passionately about that. Excitement really turns me on. It's both a positive and a negative. It helps me tremendously in my profession. However, I guess it's hard for other people to live with on a day to day basis.

***

Recognizing people's differences and respecting them. Okay, this person is obsessive-compulsive and what's important to that person may not be important to me. But if it's my boss, I'd better recognize what is important to my boss and respect that. Otherwise I may be fired.

***

275

My husband has just found out that he has ADD, through our 12-year-old son being diagnosed. He coaches my daughter's soccer team. Parents of the players can be quite sensitive to criticism and my husband can be quite intense. He cares so much about this little soccer team. Now 10-year-olds might not always hear you or do what you say, and so my husband can become intense. He'll get so intense in the game: "I said to move up!" If he has to say it again, it gets more intense—he's screaming it. And others are taking it as a criticism. He is so focused and intense that he doesn't realize the impact of his words. In fact some of the parents were talking about his coaching techniques being bad and everything. He took it to heart. He felt bad, he felt so bad that he was going to quit. He was going to quit coaching.

***

My son has ADD and he often comes across as aggressive when he is advocating for somebody else when he feels that there has been an injustice. His idealism is fine, but he's not doing it in a way that is effective to solve the problem or in a way that is going to reflect well on him. Instead of trying to mediate or negotiate, he's coming across as [saying], "This is really bad." He needs to learn how to mediate differences for a win-win instead of all or nothing.

***

I have a girlfriend who can talk to you nonstop for 20 minutes. If you interject something, [she says], "You've just cut me off. You just interrupted me." And I'm thinking, I'm just an audience, so forget it.

276

***

It seems that many of these social skills actually refer to social norms—that there is a different norm for different situations that you are in. As I was thinking about this, what occurred to me is that most people try to meet a lowest common dominator. They won't go beyond a certain limit. . . . They look at the cues and they can adjust their actions . . . in order to stay close to the norm. Maybe the fact that the norm changes from place to place and the fact that ADDers aren't real good at picking up on the cues may have something to do with it. It seems like social skills are actually a reaction to the norm.

How do you determine that you are violating a social skill rule?

I have the same thing that you talked about with your son, Jarryd with no phone ringing. And at some point I realized that I was making all the calls for lunch at work and that no one was calling me. And then I began to ask myself why. Maybe I was talking too much, and they didn't want to just sit there and listen to me.

***

Subtle verbal prompts like "Shut up, I can't listen anymore!"

***

People will give me funny looks.

277

***

Spouse's elbow in the ribs , verbal comments, or the first finger pause sign.

***

Facial expressions. I'm a visual learner so I notice if they give me some facial expression. The roll of the eyes, a turn of the head, something.

***

Or they turn around and start another conversation— that's direct!

***

It's the spouse turning to you and saying, "Calm down, calm down," and that drives me crazy. It's not good because they tell you so often. I used to be offended. But it's less now because I realize that it is what I'm doing.

How have you been successful working on improving your social skills?

In my home what we do—since there are five of us with ADD— we understand now that the person with ADD talking, likes to keep on talking but the others have short listening spans. And we'll just say, "I'm at that point." Which is a nice way to

278

say that we've reached our limit. But it's not like you're talking too much, it's like I've had all I can handle. We're not pointing fingers or discounting what they are saying. I want to hear you, but I can only take it in small chunks. Tell me the rest later. Or after a few minutes or something.

***

Just the other day I was looking for these papers and I knew that I had just had them. I was going through my piles and I can't find these papers. And my husband was yapping at me about something else. And I told him, "Right now the only thing on my mind is finding these papers, and I am not hearing anything that you are saying." So I liked her way of dealing with so many people in the family so that they don't become defensive by saying that you're at this limit right now rather than blaming the other person.

***

Having others tell me, "I can't listen anymore." That feels very nice when someone says that. Then it's on them, it's not on you.

***

Knowing what to do is important. Because I have such difficulty in this area, I would like to study the mechanics and techniques of socializing. I won't expect to be able to get it right the first time. But, if I know what to look for, I can develop a coping mechanism that will work for my unique goal in a given situation.

279

***

Change a "do or die," "all or nothing" attitude to a win-win situation. Learn to mediate differences.

***

I learn social skills from watching others and trying to figure out what they are doing right or what they are doing wrong.

***

I've had a problem with interrupting all my life. I recognized it a couple of years ago. One of the things that I do now is if someone is talking to me and I know a story that fits right in or it reminds me of something, I'll say, "Remind me to tell you about something that happened last night," and then let them continue their story. And I do that because I'll forget what I wanted to say and this way they can remind me at the end, "Tell me what you did last night." . . . And so I don't run the risk of forgetting what I wanted to say, but I also don't interrupt their story.

***

Look around. Look away from whatever place your mind is occupying and observe the faces of the people around you, as an actor or orator would do with his/her audience. Without saying a word, they are telling you what to do next.

280

***

Being funny has saved me in many social situations.

***

A woman wrote: *Working with men helped me talk less. I found that they don't like details first. They like the bottom line. It makes me more aware of getting to the point.*

***

Noticing when kids are doing the right social skill helps me become more aware of what I am doing.

***

I think that there is a sense of immediacy that ADD people have. They have to get it out right now. And their ability to tolerate that frustration is just not there. Learning to relax and say, "It's okay, I can wait ten seconds to get this out." Or I am feeling this anxiety, this is my sense of immediacy that I have to have this done or out of my mouth right now.

Being able to identify that, slow yourself down, and recognize that the words are still going to be there. Or maybe they're not. But that's okay. Develop the ability to tolerate that anxiety.

***

I think what I did to try to compensate for all the interrupting I did was try to be the life of the party. So when I would interrupt I would interrupt with a really good story. So that when everybody laughs, it was okay to interrupt.

281

***

When I talk I try to get people to laugh. I know that it's one of my coping skills for having ADD and feeling like I didn't fit in, but I find that it's hard for me to stop. And I know that I should. I can't stop. . . And I see it in my son. He's doing the same thing—being a clown.

Using humor as a defense. You're not going to like me for who I really am, so I have to make everybody laugh.

***

Keep emotion out of the way when you are trying to give helpful feedback.

***

Watch the timing. My personal preference is private. Don't tell me I'm interrupting in public. Wait and tell me in private. Now I'll even ask my wife, "How did I do tonight?"

***

I get the nudge from my spouse. I also have close associates with the ability to let me know because they know what I am dealing with. I have invited them to give me feedback. That helps me in my work environment.

***

Using the computer for on-line conversations can be very helpful in learning about the give-and-take of conversations in a relaxed setting and at your own pace. You can respond a little later—it doesn't have to be the instant response, as in most conversations. It gives space to allow you to learn how to communicate more effectively.

***

I find it helpful to [write down] the things to work on. . . . And say it in a positive way. Just like the old saying, "If you can't say anything positive don't say anything at all."

***

Brainwashing is what I call it. Before we go somewhere, I reaffirm the rules. Remember to be polite. If you are not polite, you won't be invited back. I have a list of about 10 things before going somewhere to help prompt him to act more socially appropriate.

***

My mother hasn't been diagnosed as ADD, but I'm absolutely convinced that she has it just like everyone else in my family. I have learned a lot about myself by observing her and being embarrassed by her. Like in a restaurant when she tells the waitress our family's life history. I want to tell her, "She doesn't care, mom, can't you see?" And when I'm in another social setting and there's another ADD person and

283

they're talking excessively, I know how I feel. And I get offended by it and so I guess that I have learned by observing other behavior that is similar and saying, "I hope I don't do that." And I try very hard not to.

Conclusion

I began this book talking about my son, and I'll end it the same way. Jarryd has made a lot of progress since we first began on this journey. I would love to tell you that Jarryd has impeccable social skills, but he's now 13 and that's not *exactly* the case—but he's getting there. I can tell you that by working on his social skills very intentionally he has been able to make a few friends, go over to some people's houses, go to parties, and even sleep over at some friend's houses. This is a major improvement from where we started!

Working with Jarryd has helped me better understand the concerns of the adults with AD/HD who I work with. I have also been fortunate enough to have a number of adults with AD/HD enter my life and be willing to try out new ideas and strategies. I didn't always know what I was doing, but I knew what I wanted to try. And they were willing to try as well. Together we learned many things about adult AD/HD. I am also thankful for the many adults from all around the country who have shared their struggles and triumphs with me at workshops and lectures. Their stories and ideas are a constant source of encouragement.

Although it's important to look inside yourself for affirmation, and not rely on affirmation from others, it's also important to interact in a manner that does not isolate or alienate you from others. You need to find a balance. I hope this book has given you some ideas and tools for improving your social skills and your interpersonal relationships to help you find that balance.

Most of all, I hope this book has provided you with the hope and encouragement you need as you try to improve your social situation. I hope you no longer feel that everybody else knows the secret of social skills and you don't. Now you know the secret, too.

APPENDIX A

- 20 Tips for Those Who Want to Help

- Social Skills Checklist—Self Report

- Social Skills Checklist—Observations of Others

20 Tips For Those
Who Want To Help

By special request from many of adults with AD/HD I have known, I have compiled some ideas for helpers to become more effective helpers.

1. **Is your help wanted?** Before you begin to try to help, make sure that your support and help is desired. Unwanted help is not helpful and will leave you both very frustrated.

2. **Get feedback**. Ask for feedback on you helping style. *Is this helping you? In what ways can I help you better?*

3. **Be flexible**. If your style or manner of helping isn't working, be prepared to change. After all if your help is not helping— it's not help. Be open to adjusting your style to best meet their needs.

4. **Clarification**. Due to the blinks and blanks of AD/HD pieces of information may be missed. Learn to always ask for clarification. Ask the person to repeat any directions or instructions that you have given to make sure that they have been heard in their entirety and correctly. *What did you hear me say?* This is the number one, best thing you can do to avoid misunderstandings!

5. **Clarify.** Clarify what you heard them say if you are confused. With AD/HD sometimes things don't always come out the way they should. Rather than wonder or becoming upset—ask for clarification, *I think what I just heard you say was…. Is that right?*

6. **Notice don't evaluate**. Rather than focus on the negative *You did this wrong* it's better to use phrases such as, *I noticed…* or *Are you aware that…* these wordings feel much less blaming and shaming. Telling the truth in love is important, but it is HOW you tell it that makes or breaks relationships.

7. **Timing.** Make sure the time is right to give critical feedback. Make sure that you are not rushed so that you can respond supportively. When someone is tired or just coming home from work is not generally the best time to begin with helpful feedback.

8. **Pace you feedback**. Don't overload. No one needs to hear all 58 things that they did wrong and need to work on at once. Anywhere from 1 to 3 things is more than enough at any one time. Any more can overwhelm and discourage.

9. **Confidentiality.** Be careful not to embarrass the person by giving helpful suggestions in front of others. Privacy and discretion are what is needed.

10. **Signals.** In order to converse in a public setting without embarrassment, develop some signals or cues (physical signals, like patting your hair, or rubbing your nose… verbal cues like *so..*). Work together to

develop your secret language so that you can communicate in public and hopefully help to stop social mistakes in their tracks.

11. **Sandwich** feedback with praise. Psychologists have said that we need at least seven affirmations in order to best hear one critical comment. Even if you just begin and end with affirmation (make a feedback cookie: praise— critical comment— praise) that should help.

12. **Praise**, encouragement and positive reinforcement. Most of us think that we offer praise much more frequently than we actually do. Work on increasing your affirming comments. Notice when they make a step forward and tell them! Try to catch the person doing something well. Be sincere. Written praise or notes of encouragement are great! People can read them over and over. Try to give written encouragement at times. [One trick to help you remember to offer praise is to keep 10 pennies in one pocket. Each time you offer praise, move one penny to the other pocket. See how many times you were actually able to offer praise. Don't wait till the end of the night and say 10 nice things—that's cheating!]

13. **Expectations**. With their permission, help them set *reasonable and reachable* expectations. Often with AD/HD there is a flurry of ideas and a flurry of enthusiasm. Since there are also difficulties with perception of time, they may not fully understand the time commitments involved in tasks they are select-

ing to accomplish. Help them to set reasonable goals so that they can be successful.

This is where your understanding of tasks and time will come in handy. You don't want to dampen their initiative but you also don't want them to become discouraged with failure. *You know it sounds like you are real excited about painting your whole house and writing a report this week. I'm wondering how it would be best to break those down into smaller steps to help you reach your goals. How long do you think it will take you to paint one room? What all is involved?* Ask questions to help them see that they can't do everything that they would like to all in a week.

You may also need to help prioritize goals. Sometimes everything looks equally important or appealing. Help focus attention on the urgent and important.

When they come to the realization that they need to revise their goals, help them pick a smaller part of their goal. *What do you think about setting a goal to have the family room painted by the end of the week and an abstract of the report written also by the end of the week?*

14. **Prepare**. Help the person prepare for upcoming situations. Advanced preparation can smooth the way for success. *You know we are going to a party at Carol's house, try to ask her about her new job. She's real excited about it.*

15. Strategy. With their permission, help them develop a strategy or game plan to effectively meet their goal. *Would you like for me to help you think this project through a little bit?* Help them brainstorm through the different steps and materials required as well as different ways to meet their goals.

16. Things to never say. If they fail you are not allowed to say, *I told you so.* Or *You should have done it my way.* Any of these kinds of messages make the other person feel badly. They do nothing to motivate the person to try a different way. Eliminate evaluative comments from your vocabulary. All the should's, must's, and the like need to go. *That's wrong...,That's bad...*, or *That's so stupid* have no place in a supportive relationship.

17. Offer support. If they fail, offer them support, *That must be very disappointing for you to not have met your goal.* After empathizing, you are then in a position to help them rethink their strategy. *I'm wondering where you go from here.* Hopefully this will provide the support and motivation for the person to try again.

18. Don't rescue unless absolutely necessary. Many people learn very effectively from their mistakes and failures. If people are rescued from the consequences of their action or inaction, they may never to motivated to change their behavior. Your help may actually hinder their growth.

293

19. Empathize. Try to understand the situation through the eyes of the person with AD/HD. There's an old Indian saying, *Don't judge a man until you have walked a mile in their moccasins.* This perspective will help you to be less judgmental, more compassionate and more understanding.

20. Stay neutral. Although your role is that of an encourager, try to remain emotionally neutral. Remember that this is the person's with AD/HD's goal. This is their life. Try not to get too emotional about their progress or lack of progress. If you're over emotional that actually adds additional stress in the life of the person with AD/HD. Rather than being able to turn to you for support, they may want to avoid you, because they don't want to disappoint you. They are already emotional about this!

Novotni Social Skills Checklist—Self Report

Traits

How many of the following traits of highly likeable people are descriptive of you? Circle all that apply. Put a check by the ones you would like to work on:

sincere	honest	understanding	loyal
truthful	trustworthy	intelligent	warm
thoughtful	considerate	reliable	kind
responsible	friendly	unselfish	trustful
humorous	cheerful	dependable	

Use the following checklist to identify strengths as well as areas to work on.

NOT A PROBLEM	NEEDS IMPROVEMENT	
		BASIC MANNERS: The ability to do the following in your social interactions with others.
_____	_____	• Use mannerly words like please, thank you, and you're welcome
_____	_____	• Express appreciation
_____	_____	• Receive compliments without discounting
_____	_____	• Give compliments regularly to others
_____	_____	• Apologize
_____	_____	• Accept the apology of others
_____	_____	• Introduce yourself
_____	_____	• Introduce others
_____	_____	• Use appropriate greetings
_____	_____	• Use appropriate ending comments
_____	_____	• Phone manners
_____	_____	• Mealtime behaviors (follow lead of host/hostess, chew with mouth closed, don't talk when mouth full, ask to have items passed, use napkins, elbows off the table, ask to be excused)
_____	_____	• Making others feel comfortable in your home—hosting
_____	_____	• Offer to help others

Note: From Michele Novotni, *What Does Everybody Else Know That I Don't?* Copyright 1999 by Specialty Press, Inc. This form may be reproduced for personal use. For professional use please order copies from A.D.D. WareHouse, 300 NW 70th Ave., Plantation, Fl 33317, (800) 233-9273.

NOT A PROBLEM	NEEDS IMPROVEMENT	
		II. VERBAL COMMUNICATION SKILLS:
		In conversation with others the ability to:
_____	_____	• Join a conversation without disruption
_____	_____	• Check—repeat what you heard and ask if you heard it right
_____	_____	• Identify and reflect *content* of conversation—tracking
_____	_____	• Identify and reflect *feelings* of others
_____	_____	• Ability to reflect content + feelings in conversations
_____	_____	• Use minimal encouragers to let others know you are following the conversation
_____	_____	• Use open questions to keep conversations going
_____	_____	• Ask for help when needed or desired

III. NONVERBAL COMMUNICATION SKILLS: Looking attentive when listening. When talking with others do you:

NOT A PROBLEM	NEEDS IMPROVEMENT	
_____	_____	• Keep an open posture
_____	_____	• Face the person
_____	_____	• Lean forward
_____	_____	• Maintain appropriate eye contact
_____	_____	• Look relaxed

IV. COMMUNICATION ROADBLOCKS

NOT A PROBLEM	NEEDS IMPROVEMENT	
_____	_____	• Miss pieces of information—"blinks"
_____	_____	• Use closed or naked questions
_____	_____	• Voice too loud or too soft
_____	_____	• Speak too quickly
_____	_____	• Interrupt others
_____	_____	• Too quiet—rarely speaking in conversations
_____	_____	• Talk excessively
_____	_____	• Order or boss others
_____	_____	• Critical—judge or evaluate others
_____	_____	• Minimize or not be considerate

V. ORGANIZATIONAL SKILLS—TRUSTWORTHY

NOT A PROBLEM	NEEDS IMPROVEMENT	
_____	_____	• Difficulty with deadlines
_____	_____	• Difficulty being on time for meetings and appointments

296

NOT A PROBLEM	NEEDS IMPROVEMENT	
_____	_____	• Dificulty remembering special occasions
_____	_____	• Too organized, rigid
_____	_____	• Difficulty managing money, bills, bank accounts, etc.
_____	_____	• Difficulty organizing your stuff
_____	_____	• Do what you agree to do
_____	_____	• Finish projects

VI. SELF CONTROL

_____	_____	• Take turns/wait
_____	_____	• Ability to handle inappropriate behavior of others
_____	_____	• Effectively manage conflict, negotiate and compromise
_____	_____	• Effectively manage anger
_____	_____	• Refrain from aggressive behavior
_____	_____	• Assertiveness
_____	_____	• Impulsive spending
_____	_____	• Impulsive decision-making
_____	_____	• Filter thoughts avoiding impulsive words—blurting things that hurt people
_____	_____	• Inappropriate touch of others
_____	_____	• Difficulty relaxing
_____	_____	• Excessive physical activity (trouble staying seated, fidget, feeling restless)

VII. KNOWLEDGE

_____	_____	• Understand *attribution theory*'s role in social relationships
_____	_____	• Understand the importance of *social exchange theory*—give and take in relationships
_____	_____	• Understand the subtle cues that you give others with your body language
_____	_____	• Ability to pick up the *subtext*—socially perceptive
_____	_____	• Understand *context*

VIII. RELATIONSHIPS

_____	_____	• Sensitive to the needs of others
_____	_____	• Patient
_____	_____	• Creative

297

NOT A PROBLEM	NEEDS IMPROVEMENT	
_____	_____	• Fun to be with
_____	_____	• Flexible—able to go with the flow
_____	_____	• Respect boundary of others
_____	_____	• Treat others with respect
_____	_____	• Tolerance to differences of others
_____	_____	• Initiate invitations to others
_____	_____	• Difficulty with intimacy
_____	_____	• Have at least three close friends

IX. SELF CARE

NOT A PROBLEM	NEEDS IMPROVEMENT	
_____	_____	• Ability to nurture yourself
_____	_____	• Appearance—clean, neat, and appropriate for situations
_____	_____	• Ability to identify and express your feelings
_____	_____	• Self-esteem
_____	_____	• Participate in support groups
_____	_____	• Sense of humor
_____	_____	• Positive outlook—hope

What is the most important area for you to work on to improve your social relationships?

_____ Basic Manners

_____ Verbal Communication Skills

_____ Nonverbal Communication Skills

_____ Communication Roadblocks

_____ Organizational Skills

_____ Self Control

_____ Knowledge

_____ Relationships

_____ Self Care

Novotni Social Skills Checklist–Observations of Others

Traits

How many of the following traits of highly likeable people are descriptive? Circle all that apply. Put a check by the ones you would like to see him/her work on:

sincere	honest	understanding	loyal
truthful	trustworthy	intelligent	warm
thoughtful	considerate	reliable	kind
responsible	friendly	unselfish	trustful
humorous	cheerful	dependable	

Use the following checklist to identify strengths as well as areas to work on that you have observed. Leave item blank if not observed.

NOT A PROBLEM	NEEDS IMPROVEMENT	
		BASIC MANNERS: The ability to do the following in their social interactions with others.
_____	_____	• Use mannerly words like please, thank you, and you're welcome
_____	_____	• Express appreciation
_____	_____	• Receive compliments without discounting
_____	_____	• Give compliments regularly to others
_____	_____	• Apologize
_____	_____	• Accept the apology of others
_____	_____	• Introduce himself/herself to others
_____	_____	• Introduce others
_____	_____	• Use appropriate greetings
_____	_____	• Use appropriate ending comments
_____	_____	• Phone manners
_____	_____	• Mealtime behaviors (follow lead of host/hostess, chew with mouth closed, don't talk when mouth full, ask to have items passed, use napkins, elbows off the table, ask to be excused)
_____	_____	• Making others feel comfortable in their home—hosting
_____	_____	• Offer to help others

NOT A PROBLEM	NEEDS IMPROVEMENT	
		II. VERBAL COMMUNICATION SKILLS: In conversation with others the ability to:
___	___	• Join a conversation without disruption
___	___	• Check—repeat what they heard and ask if they heard it right
___	___	• Identify and reflect *content* of conversation—tracking
___	___	• Identify and reflect *feelings* of others
___	___	• Ability to reflect content + feelings in conversations
___	___	• Use minimal encouragers to let others know they are following the conversation
___	___	• Use open questions to keep conversations going
___	___	• Ask for help when needed or desired

III. NONVERBAL COMMUNICATION SKILLS: Looking attentive when listening. When talking with others does he/she:

NOT A PROBLEM	NEEDS IMPROVEMENT	
___	___	• Keep an open posture
___	___	• Face the person
___	___	• Lean forward
___	___	• Maintain appropriate eye contact
___	___	• Look relaxed

IV. COMMUNICATION ROADBLOCKS

NOT A PROBLEM	NEEDS IMPROVEMENT	
___	___	• Miss pieces of information—"blinks"
___	___	• Use closed or naked questions
___	___	• Voice too loud or too soft
___	___	• Speak too quickly
___	___	• Interrupt others
___	___	• Too quiet—rarely speaking in conversations
___	___	• Talk excessively
___	___	• Order or boss others
___	___	• Critical—judge or evaluate others
___	___	• Minimize or not be considerate

V. ORGANIZATIONAL SKILLS—TRUSTWORTHY

NOT A PROBLEM	NEEDS IMPROVEMENT	
___	___	• Difficulty with deadlines
___	___	• Difficulty being on time for meetings and appointments

300

NOT A PROBLEM	NEEDS IMPROVEMENT	
_____	_____	• Dificulty remembering special occasions
_____	_____	• Too organized, rigid
_____	_____	• Difficulty managing money, bills, bank accounts, etc.
_____	_____	• Difficulty organizing their stuff
_____	_____	• Do what they agree to do
_____	_____	• Finish projects

VI. SELF CONTROL

_____	_____	• Take turns/wait
_____	_____	• Ability to handle inappropriate behavior of others
_____	_____	• Effectively manage conflict, negotiate and compromise
_____	_____	• Effectively manage anger
_____	_____	• Refrain from aggressive behavior
_____	_____	• Assertiveness
_____	_____	• Impulsive spending
_____	_____	• Impulsive decision-making
_____	_____	• Filter thoughts avoiding impulsive words—blurting things that hurt people
_____	_____	• Inappropriate touch of others
_____	_____	• Difficulty relaxing
_____	_____	• Excessive physical activity (trouble staying seated, fidget, feeling restless)

VII. KNOWLEDGE

_____	_____	• Understand *attribution theory*'s role in social relationships
_____	_____	• Understand the importance of *social exchange theory*—give and take in relationships
_____	_____	• Understand the subtle cues that they give others with their body language
_____	_____	• Ability to pick up the *subtext*—socially perceptive
_____	_____	• Understand *context*

VIII. RELATIONSHIPS

_____	_____	• Sensitive to the needs of others
_____	_____	• Patient
_____	_____	• Creative

301

NOT A PROBLEM	NEEDS IMPROVEMENT	
_____	_____	• Fun to be with
_____	_____	• Flexible—able to go with the flow
_____	_____	• Respect boundary of others
_____	_____	• Treat others with respect
_____	_____	• Tolerance to differences of others
_____	_____	• Initiate invitations to others
_____	_____	• Difficulty with intimacy
_____	_____	• Have at least three close friends

IX. SELF CARE

NOT A PROBLEM	NEEDS IMPROVEMENT	
_____	_____	• Ability to nurture him/herself
_____	_____	• Appearance—clean, neat, and appropriate for situations
_____	_____	• Ability to identify and express feelings
_____	_____	• Self-esteem
_____	_____	• Participate in support groups
_____	_____	• Sense of humor
_____	_____	• Positive outlook—hope

In your opinion, what is the most important area for this person to work on to improve social relationships?

_____ Basic Manners

_____ Verbal Communication Skills

_____ Nonverbal Communication Skills

_____ Communication Roadblocks

_____ Organizational Skills

_____ Self Control

_____ Knowledge

_____ Relationships

_____ Self Care

302

Bibliography

Books

Barkley, R. (1990). *Attention deficit-hyperactivity disorder: A handbook for diagnosis and treatment.* New York: Guilford Press.

Barkley, R. (1997). *ADHD and the nature of self-control.* New York: Guilford Press.

Begun, R. W., (Ed.). (1996). *Social Skills Lessons & Activities for Grades 7-12.* New York: The Center for Applied Research in Education.

Braswell, L., & Bloomquist, M. (1991). *Cognitive-behavioral therapy with ADHD children: Child, family, and school interventions.* New York: Guilford Press

Covey, S. (1989). *The 7 habits of highly effective people.* New York: Simon and Schuster.

Egan, G. (1998). *The skilled helper: A problem-management approach to helping. (6th ed.). Pacific Grove, California:* Brooks/Cole Publishing Company.

Elias, M.J., & Tobias, S.E. (1996) *Social problem-solving: interventions in the schools.* New York: Guilford Press.

Elksnin, L., & Elksnin, N. (1995). *Assessment and instruction of social skills. (2nd ed.). San Diego:* Singular Publishing Group, Inc.

Fulghum, R. (1988). *All I really need to know I learned in kindergarten: Uncommon thoughts on common things.* *New York:* Ivy Books

Frankel, F. (1996). *Good friends are hard to find.* Los Angeles: Perspective Publishing.

Fowler, R. (1995). *Honey, are you listening.* Nasville, TN: Thomas Nelson Publishers.

Goleman, D. (1995). *Emotional intelligence.* New York: Bantam Books

Goldstein, S., & Goldstein, M. (1998). *Managing attention deficit hyperactivity disorder in children.* New York: John Wiley & Sons, Inc.

Gresham, F., & Elliott, S. (1993). *Social skills intervention guide: Systematic approaches to social skills training.* Binghamton, New York: The Haworth Press, Inc.

Guevremont, D. (1990). Social skills and peer relationship training. In R.A. Barkley, *Attention deficit-hyperactivity disorder: A handbook for diagnosis and treatment.* New York: Guilford Press.

Halverstadt, J. (1998). *A.D.D. and romance: Finding fulfillment in love, sex, & relationships.* Dallas: Taylor Publishing Company.

Hallowell, E., & Ratey, J. (1994) *Driven to distraction.* New York: Pantheon Books.

Khalsa, S. (1996). *Group exercises for enhancing social skills and self-Eesteem.* Sarasota, Florida: Professional Resource Press.

Lerner, H. (1989). *The dance of intimacy.* New York: Harper & Row.

Luquet, W., & Hannah, M. T. (Ed.) (1998). *Healing in the relational paradigm.* Washington, D.C.: Taylor & Francis.

Osman, B. (1982). *No one to play with: The social side of learning disabilities.* New York: Random House.

Sheridan, S. (1997). *The tough kid social skills book.* Longmont, Colorado: Sopris West.

Sheridan, S. (1998). *Why don't they like me? Helping your child make and keep friends.* Longmont, Colorado: Sopris West.

Sprafkin, R., Gershaw, N. J., & Goldstein, A. (1993). *Social skill For mental health: A structured learning approach.* Needham Heights, Massachusetts: Allyn and Bacon.

Taylor, S., Peplau, L., & Sears, D. (1997). *Social psychology (9th ed.).* Upper Saddle River, New Jersey: Prentice Hall.

Weiss, L. (1992). *Attention deficit disorder in adults: Practical help and understanding.* Dallas: Taylor Publishing Co.

Whiteman, T., & Novotni, M. (1995). *Adult ADD: A reader-friendly guide to identifying, understanding, and treating adult attention deficit disorder.* Colorado Springs, Colorado: Pinion Press.

Video Tapes

Amen, D. (1995). *A.D.D. in intimate relationships: Problems and solutions for couples affected by A.D.D.*, Fairfield, California: MindWorks Press.

Lavoie, R. (1994). *Learning disabilities and social skills: Last one picked.. first one picked on.* Washington, D.C.: WETA-TV

Audio Cassettes

Mills, J. (1993). *Urgent reply.* Marquette, Michigan: BOOM-ZING.

Journal Articles

Brown, B., Hedinger, T., & Mieling, G. (1995). The power in universality of experience: A homogeneous group approach to social skills training for individuals with learning disabilities. *The Journal for Specialists in Group Work, 20,* 98-107.

Carrol, A., Bain, A., & Houghton, S. (1994). The efects of interactive versus linear video on the levels of attention and comprehension of social behavior by children with attention disorders. *School Psychology Review, 23,* 29-43.

Chalk, M., & Smith, H. (1995). Training professionals to run social skills groups for children. *Educational Psychology in Practice, 11*, 30 - 36.

Cousins, L., & Weiss, G. (1993). Parent training and social skills training for children with attention-deficit hyperactivity disorder: How can they be combined for greater effectiveness? *Canadian Journal of Psychiatry, 38,* 449-457.

Erwin, P. (1994). Effectiveness of social skills training with children: A meta-analytic study. *Counseling Psychology Quarterly, 7,* 305-310.

Forness, S., & Kavale, K. (1996). Treating social skill deficits in children with learning disabilities: A metoanalysis of the research. *Learning Disability Quarterly, 19,* 2- 13.

Frankel, F., Myatt, R., & Cantwell, D. (1995). Training outpatient boys to conform with the social ecology of popular peers: Effects on parent and teacher ratings. *Journal of Clinical Child Psychology, 24*, 300-310.

Frederick, B., & Olmi, J. (1994). Children with attention - deficit/ hyperactive disorder: A review of the literature on social skills deficits. *Psychology in the Schools, 31,* 288 - 295.

Gresham, F. (1994). Generalization of social skills: Risks of choosing form over function. *School Psychology Quarterly, 9,* 142-144.

Kolko, D., Loar, L., & Sturnick, D. (1990). Inpatient social-cognitive skills training groups with conduct disordered children. *Journal of Child Psychiatry, 31,* 737-748.

Landau, S., & Moore, L. (1991). Social skill deficits in children with attention-deficit hyperactivity disorder. *School Psychology Review, 20(2),* 235-251.

Lenhart, L., & Rabiner, D. (1995). An integrative approach to the study of social competence in adolescence. *Development and Psychopathology, 7,* 543-561.

Margalit, M. (1995). Social skills learning for students with learning disabilities and students with behavior disorders. *Educational Psychology, 15,* 445- 456.

Muscott, H., & Gifford, T. (1994). Virtual reality and social skills training for students with behavioral disorders: Applications, Challenges and Promising Practices. *Education and Treatment of Children, 17,* 417-434.

Sheridan, S., Dee, C., Morgan, J., McCormick, M., & Walker, D. (1996). A multimethod intervention for social skills deficits in children with ADHD and their parents. *School Psychology Review, 25,* 57-76.

Teeter, P. (1997). Building social skills in children with ADD: A multimodal approach, *ATTENTION!, Summer,* 16 - 20.

Wright, N. (1995). Social skills training for conduct-disordered boys in residential treatment: A promising approach. *Residential Treatment for Children & Youth, 12(4),* 15-28.

Assessment Products

Novotni, M. (1999). *Novotni Social Skills Checklist—Self-Report Version.* Plantation, Florida: Specialty Press, Inc. Available through A.D.D. WareHouse (800) 233-9273.

Novotni, M. (1999). *Novotni Social Skills Checklist—Observer Report Version.* Plantation, Florida: Specialty Press, Inc. Available through A.D.D. WareHouse (800) 233-9273.

Index